Saint Louis
TREASURES

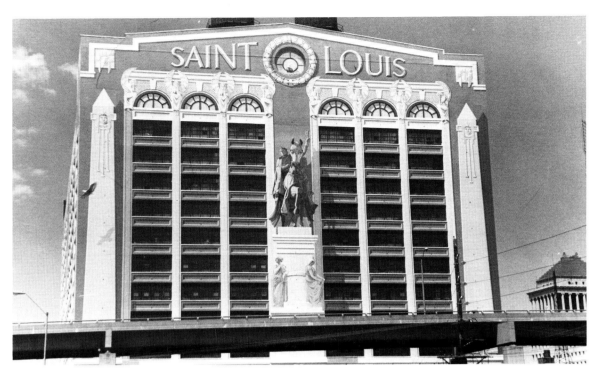

Murals:
Edison Brothers Distribution Center, Fourteenth
and Spruce Streets.
Artist: Richard Haas.

Photographs and Text By

ELINOR MARTINEAU

Saint Louis TREASURES

"Art gives nothing but the highest quality to your moments as they pass ..."

Walter Pater

COYLE

THE FOLKESTONE PRESS • SAINT LOUIS, MISSOURI

ISBN: 0-910600-08-9
Library of Congress Catalog Card Number: 85-080553

Printed in the United States of America
by the Messenger Printing Company, Kirkwood, Missouri.

To Charles,

Denise and Michael

Other Books By The Same Author

OLD SAINT LOUIS HOMES 1764-1865: THE STORIES THEY TELL

SAINT LOUIS HOMES 1866-1916: THE GOLDEN AGE

SAINT LOUIS: PORTRAIT OF A RIVER CITY

IN COLLABORATION:

The Cupples House: A Turn Of The Century Romanesque Mansion (M. McNamee, S.J.)

Short Footsteps On A Long Journey: The Poetry of Chan Sei Gow (Robert Miller)

Little Pierre (Carol Perkins)

Remembering The Saint Louis World's Fair (Margaret Witherspoon)

Author's Note

When the first edition of my first book, *Old Saint Louis Homes: The Stories They Tell,* was published in 1964 (there have been seven editions since) only a relatively small number of people were aware—or cared—about the city's wealth of architecture. For not much had ever been made of it. And what is not known is of small consequence. To illustrate: my first lecture-to-be on historic Saint Louis homes was cancelled for—so the program chairman explained to me—"No one is interested in old houses."

Times have changed. A lot. The heritage homes of Saint Louis and the surrounding area now receive a great deal of appreciative attention. It seems to be a valid claim that Saint Louis is one of the leaders in the nation in the restoration and rehabilitation of old houses. And it had been my privilege (and joy) to have been in the vanguard of those who touted the uniqueness and abundance of Saint Louis' rich architectural legacy.

But in wandering about Saint Louis over the years so many other treasures have come to my attention. Architectural gems; religious objects of considerable value, historic interest or beauty; art objects, some venerable with age, some important to our history, some just beautiful. Some are well known. Some are not. But they all share one common denominator. The colorful stories they tell are often overlooked if not entirely forgotten.

So this book has more or less been forced upon me by a nagging conscience to call attention to some of these treasures. Treasures that make living in Saint Louis such a pleasure. And hopefully, to motivate others to make their own discoveries. For that is half of the fun. But there is so much to savour; to enjoy; that is entertaining plus mind-enriching. And any or all will add an extra fillip to life.

Elinor Martineau Coyle

Gates to Vandeventer Place, all that remains from what was once the grandest of all the Private Places of Saint Louis. (Gates now near Jewel Box in Forest Park.)

Acknowledgements

Many people have been both gracious and helpful to me in my gathering of material and taking of photographs for **Saint Louis Treasures**. To all of them, my heartfelt thanks.

And a very special "thank you" to Reinhardt Stiegemeier who developed my pictures; and to Herbert Jones and Carol Vance of Messenger Printing Company for their suggestions, support and patience in bringing this book to completion.

One of the four majestic eagles decorating the roof of the Jefferson Memorial Building, home of the Missouri Historical Society.
Sculptor: Karl Bitter.

Foreword

Metropolitan Saint Louis is a veritable treasure house of many unseen and unappreciated artistic, historical and cultural features and resources. For most of the area's residents are not specifically looking for these objects, and the stories behind those that they do notice are largely unknown. As a result most of these treasures are either missed completely or overlooked as citizens go about their daily lives.

To help Saint Louisans in locating and understanding the rich resources found all around us, Elinor Martineau Coyle has devoted herself to finding and explaining these interesting features of our city's heritage. Her critical eye has ranged over the entire landscape of the built environment for these special objects which most of us miss. She has spent many years studying the community's past and present and her writings and talks have both enlightened and piqued the curiosity of her readers and listeners.

In this volume one will find that Saint Louis is filled with innumerable pieces of public art, statues, markers, numerous architectural features and details, and many whimsical objects which become startling when their stories are known.

Mrs. Coyle invites her readers to use this book on several levels of personal enjoyment. The many photographs reveal various features that are often missed entirely by others; and her narrative contains details not readily known concerning countless of these treasures. Readers will also find the volume an invaluable guide in touring the metro area to experience first hand individual parts of our cultural tapestry. They will find this work sharpening both their personal perception and understanding of Saint Louis' past and present. It is a volume that I believe adds greatly to the historical record of our city.

Saint Louis
April, 1986

Raymond F. Pisney, Executive Director
Missouri Historical Society

Southwestern Bell Telephone Building, one of the city's newest skyscrapers
Architects: Hellmuth, Obata and Kassabaum.
In this quest for a greater understanding and appreciation of treasures from Saint Louis'
yesterdays, let us not overlook the treasures of tomorrow that are being created by the
resurgence of the Saint Louis of today.

Contents

Foreword 9

Part One: Architectural Treasures 14

Early French Architecture .... *Aubuchon House* 16

.... *Taille de Noyer* 17

Early American Houses .... *Thomas Sappington House* 18

.... *White Haven, Lyle House* 19

Greek Revival Style .... *Old Cathedral* 20

.... *Old Courthouse* 21

.... *DeMenil Mansion, Hanley House* ... 22

.... *Primm, Fishback, Meyers Houses* ... 23

.... *Holy Corners* 24

Italianate Villas .... *Oakland; Gurney House* 26

Victorian-Italianate Style .... *Franz Arzt House* 27

French Second Empire .... *Blair-Huse-Conley House* 28

.... *Obert House* 29

German Influences 30

Romanesque Style .... *Samuel Cupples House* 32

Private Places 34

Doorways 36

A Rhine Castle .... *Grant's Farm* 40

Influences from the Past .... *Masonic Temple* 42

.... *Christ Church Cathedral Altar Screen* ... 43

.... *Brookings Hall* 44

.... *Graham Chapel* 45

.... *Soulard Market, Linnean House, Warwick Vase copy* ... 46

.... *Civil Courts Building* 47

.... *Saint Francis de Sales Church* 48

.... *College Church; Saint John the Apostle*
.... * and Evangelist Church* 49

.... *Saint Louis Union Station* 50

.... *Saint Louis Public Library* 52

.... *Kirkpatrick-Ross, Shaw Town House* ... 54

.... *Zoo Wall, Armbruster Mortuary,*
.... * Williamsburg House* 55

University City Civic Buildings 56

The Brick City 58

Architectural Embellishments 60

Decorative Iron Work 62

Building Ornamentation 66

Watertowers 72

Clocks 73

Kirkwood Depot 74

Edgewood Center 75

Saint Stanislaus Museum 76

Lakewood School House, Gentry House 77

Chinese Pagoda, Tower Grove Park Ruins 78

Part Two: Public Art 79

Thomas and Anne Mullanphy Biddle High Reliefs 80

Mercantile Library Association Art Collection .... *D. Webster, Napoleon's Head, Audubon's "Birds"* ... 81

Harriet Hosmer Statues .... *Beatrice Cenci, Wayman Crow* 82

.... *Thomas Hart Benton, Ariadne* 83

Tower Grove Park Statues .... *Shakespeare* 84

.... *Columbus, Von Humboldt* 85

.... *Canova Lions, Bandstand* 86

Missouri Botanical Garden .... *Ridgway Center, Former Entrance* ... 87

.... *Fountains, Mother and Child Sculpture* ... 88

.... *Zerogee, Calder Mobiles, Linnaeus Bust* ... 89

.... *"Female," Birds in Flight* 90

.... *Japanese Garden* 91

Civil War Memorials . . . . General Nathaniel Lyon 92

General U.S. Grant 93

Frank Blair, Jr. 94

Confederate Commemorative Memorial 95

Relics from the 1904 World's Fair . . . . Louis IX Statue; Art Museum Pediment 96

Art Museum; "Sculpture" 97

Jefferson Statue; Fair Mural,

Jefferson Statue; Fair Mural, Signing of Louisiana Purchase Treaty . . . 98

Bixby Art Gallery; Jefferson Memorial Building 99

World's Fair Pavilion; John; Angel of Mercy 100

Fair Mural; Francis Field; von Steuben 101

Other Art Works . . . . Italian Immigrants 102

Naked Truth; Spanish Cannon; Washington Statue 103

"Vision," Laclede Statue, Bacchus 104

"Moby Dick;" Pius XII; Easter Island Heads 105

Burns; Blake; Bear 106

Saint Francis of Assisi 107

Fountains 108

Outdoor Wall Murals 112

Contemporary Art; "The Wall" 116

Oldenburg, Hepworth; Lipchitz 117

Saint Louis Centre; "Les Danseuses" 118

Laumeier Park 119

Gateway Arch 120

Part Three: Memorial Art at Bellefontaine 121

and Calvary Cemeteries

Henry Shreve 123

Mullanphy; McCash 124

General William Clark 125

Auguste Chouteau; Manuel Lisa 126

Stephen Kearny; William Beaumont 127

Bellefontaine Cemetery . . . . James Eads 128

Hamilton Gamble; Sterling Price; R. Mason 129

Plymouth Rock; Samuel Hawkin; Krenning 130

Teasdale; Minor; Yeatman; Bagnell 131

Griesedieck; Van Court; Protestant Memorial 132

David R. Francis; Hudson Bridges 133

Von Der Ahe; Kate Bennett 134

Isaiah Sellers; Herman Luyties 135

George Brown; Lemp Mausoleums 136

Wainwright, Busch Mausoleums 137

Calvary Cemetery . . . . Chapel; Tower 138

Pierre Chouteau Family Plot; Gratiot 139

Biddle Tomb; Kate Chopin; Gypsy Queen 140

William T. Sherman; Dred Scott 141

Thomas Dooley 142

Part Four: Religious Art Treasures 143

Saint Luke; Madonna; Festival Chair 144

Jeweled Chalice 145

Marquette's Monstrance; Bell;

Saint Ferdinand's Church

John Clark's Tombstone; Rock Hill Presbyterian Church; . . . 147

Last Supper Needlework

Fabergé Eggs 148

Church of the Ascension Tiffany Window 149

Saint Louis Cathedral 150

Pontius Pilate Mosaic 154

Ikon Head 155

Saint Elizabeth of Hungary, "Light of the World" 156

Saint Nicholas Greek Orthodox Church Sanctuary 157

Historic North and South Side Churches 158

Jewish Religious Art 160

Church Steeples 162

Modern Church Architecture 164

Miscellaneous Religious Art 168

Part Five: New Treasures from Old Treasures 171

"Thornhill," Museum of Transportation 172

Powell Hall, Fox Theatre 173

New Treasures . . . . St. Louis Centre, Smith House 174

Architectural Treasures

Gargoyle,
Washington University

Saint Louis can count amongst its existing treasures not only examples of almost every architectural style ever to be popular in the United States but a wealth of architectural ornamental embellishments as well. Fanciful iron work, handsome doorways and windows, graceful cornices and ballustrades, high reliefs, low reliefs that are also a part of this architectural legacy—and all esthetically satisfying—and that add immeasurably to the visual pleasures of the Saint Louis environment.

This is due to a number of reasons. One is the innate conservatism of Saint Louisans who look upon change for the mere sake of change with a wary eye. Another is that many of these examples are in depressed areas where no profit motive existed to tear down old buildings to make way for modern ones. Or they were in a part of the community that was not developing in a way that required the destruction of older structures. And some remain because of the dedication of concerned citizens who worked tirelessly to save a particular building that had a special significance for them.

Whatever the reason, Saint Louis and Saint Louis County still have an abundance of excellent architectural expressions from bygone eras. These help to give Saint Louis a character and personality that sets it apart from all other American cities.

Gargoyle,
Washington University

1314 South Tenth Street.
Graceful iron balconies abound in North and South Saint Louis.

There is an ancient proverb that a prophet is not without honor save in his own country. Thus it has been with Saint Louis, for its citizens were many years in realizing what a rich architectural heritage they possessed. But now, at long last, there are few who do not take pride in this magnificent legacy. And also, at long last, the city and metroplex are being recognized by national authorities as an architectural treasure trove with few peers.

900 block, Morrison Street
Restored Victorian town houses.

One Portland Place
Caryatid.

1102 Rue Saint Louis, Florissant, circa 1800. One of the relatively few local examples of the style of architecture developed by the French settlers in the Upper Mississippi Valley.

Builder unknown. Called the Auguste Aubuchon House, as the first record of the house is his purchase of it in 1844. All evidence, however, points to its being much older.

Early French Architecture

One of the most interesting aspects of the Saint Louis architectural legacy is that it traces in an orderly fashion the development of the area through the styles of architecture favored by the groups who settled here. First, of course, were the French who founded Saint Louis. In 1764 Pierre Laclede, a well-educated, well-born native of France, came up the Mississippi River with a small band of followers to establish a fur-trading post to take advantage of the monopoly rights for trading with the Indians of rich Upper Louisiana granted to him and his New Orleans partners by the French Governor-General of all the Louisiana Territory.

Over the next forty years—until the signing of the Louisiana Purchase Treaty in 1804—Saint Louis developed into a prosperous French colonial village although, due to European political machinations, it was an outpost of the Spanish Empire. The French settlers who came here were from France, New Orleans and Canada, as well as from other French colonial villages on the east side of the river. These latter not only wished to escape the English rule that was to be imposed upon them as a result of France losing all of its territories east of the Mississippi River due to the English victory in the French and Indian Wars; but were also enticed by Laclede's offer to give them land in the new village if a house was built upon it within a year—the first homestead act in this part of the world.

The homes these first Saint Louisans built were especially suitable for this climate. To shade the house during the hot summer months, a *galerie* with a steep, sloping roof that formed the ceiling, was built across the front. Sometimes these *galeries* were also on two sides or three sides—and on occasion—all four sides of the structure. Here the villagers would sit in the cool of the summer evenings to drink tafia, their favorite rum drink, and often to dance or sing to the tune of a merry fiddle, for they were a gay, light-hearted, gregarious people who loved simple pleasures.

Taille de Noyer
One Rue de Taille de Noyer
Florissant.
This section of Taille de Noyer, built in the 1790's by the French fur trader, Hycinthe Deshetres, is also typical of the Missouri-French architectural style. Additions were made to it in the early nineteenth century by the then owners, Mr. and Mrs. Charles Chambers, to accommodate their growing family (seventeen children in all). Mrs. Chambers was a daughter of John Mullanphy, Saint Louis' first millionaire, who gave the property to her as a wedding present in 1816.

In the 1960's the house was saved from demolition, moved to its present site on the McCluer High School grounds, and then restored by the Florissant Valley Historical Society. The saving of this house and subsequent publicity were influential in helping to create a new awareness for many Saint Louisans of the importance of saving some of the area's history houses as a visible link with the past.

To conserve heat in the winter, the ceilings of these French colonial houses were usually low, with a large stone fireplace at either end of the *grande salle,* the large room that extended across the front of the house. And, to take advantage of the tempering influences of the river, practically all houses in the village were built to face it.

Today little that is tangible remains from this Creole period. The devastating 1849 fire destroyed the Saint Louis river front, the site of the original village, and obliterated almost all traces of it there. Another important reason that so little has survived of this early French heritage is a total disregard of it by most of the populace, then primarily of Anglo-American or German stock, during the nineteenth century. Another equally decisive reason—this time a built-in one—was the custom of erecting these French-type houses by setting vertical logs directly into the ground. When eventual decay set in, the building was doomed.

Due to these combined circumstances, only a miniscule number of the French houses from the area's colonial period remain. These are mostly in Florissant, another early French village, now part of the Saint Louis metroplex. For Florissant, off the beaten track, was untouched by developers until after World War II when an enormous building boom was generated there by the development of the nearby McDonnell Aircraft Corporation.

By this time interest was aroused in saving some of the town's architectual heritage. The city management deserves considerable credit for its far-seeing preservation activities which have helped to preserve the town's quaintness and charm.

Thomas Sappington House
1015 South Sappington Road, Crest-
wood.
In 1805 Thomas Sappington, ac-
companying his father John, his
mother Jemmina, fifteen brothers
and sisters, along with forty other
families, migrated here from Ken-
tucky to settle. John had come the
previous year to buy 2000-acres of
land, at the going rate of a gallon of
whiskey an acre, in the southwest
part of the county (now Crestwood,
Sappington, parts of Webster Groves)
for the group.

Two-hundred arpents of land was
given to Thomas by his father when
the former was married in 1808. The
home Thomas built for his bride on
this wedding-present land is the
area's best remaining Federal-style
house, as well as probably the oldest
brick house west of the Mississippi
River. Now handsomely restored by
the City of Crestwood and the Saint
Louis County Historic Buildings
Commission, it is a popular place for
tours into the long ago.

Early American Architecture

With the arrival of the land-hungry, hard-working Americans who flocked here after the signing of the Louisiana Purchase Treaty (March 9-10, 1804) and the subsequent opening up of the West, the easy-going, pleasure-loving French were soon displaced as the dominant influence in Saint Louis. The Americans, like all conquerors from the beginning of time, brought with them their own ways along with their favorite types of architecture. The style developed by the French of the Upper Mississippi Valley, so suitable and practical for this climate, was ignored. The Americans built homes like the ones they had left behind.

Those who came from the East favored the severe Federal architecture, then in high fashion along the Eastern Seaboard. Those from the Southern States often established large plantations in the outlying sections where they built rambling, many-roomed homes to accommodate their more leisurely ways of life, which included almost endless entertaining of friends and relatives.

White Haven
9060 White Haven Drive
1808.
Another "bride-house," White Haven was built by William Lindsey Long at the time of his marriage to Elizabeth Sappington, daughter of John and Jemmina, and sister of Thomas. Long was the son of Captain John Long who brought his family to Alta Lusiana in 1797, one of the first American families to come into the territory.

In 1818 the plantation and house were purchased by Anne Lucas Hunt and her first husband, Theodore. Three years later Colonel Fred Dent, future father-in-law of Ulysses S. Grant, became its owner. It was at White Haven in 1842 that Julia Dent and Grant first met; much of their courtship took place here.

Grant bought White Haven from Dent during his presidency with the intention of eventually retiring here and raising fine horses, always one of his prime interests. However, as he lost the estate, along with almost everything else he possessed during a financial crisis in the 1880's, this plan did not come to pass.

The majority of the city and county's remaining heritage houses date from the middle years of the nineteenth century. Although in some of the outlying sections, where the burgeoning growth of the area did not require the elimination of all older buildings, a fair number of houses dating from the early 1800's are still to be found. Some have been saved and maintained by the historical society of their respective communities; some are owned by the city or county park systems; some have been turned into business offices; some are in private hands.

Alexander Lyle House circa 1840's
Location: Carondelet Park.
Confiscated from Lyle during the Civil War period because of his outspoken Confederate sympathies. Presently used for senior citizen activities.

The Basilica of Saint Louis, King of France, (Old Cathedral) was the first major example of Greek Revival architecture in Missouri. Begun in 1831, finished in 1834, its exquisite proportions were a tremendous influence in making the style popular in the entire region.

The fourth church to be erected on the site (which had been set aside by Pierre Laclede for a church in the original plans for his settlement) this is said to be the only block of land in Saint Louis which has never ᵕhanged hands since its founding.

Although once the Mother Church for Roman Catholics in over half of the United States, the old church was sadly neglected during the years that the city turned its back on the river. In 1914, when the new cathedral was dedicated, it even lost its title and became simply the Church of Saint Louis, even though it continued to be generally known as the Old Cathedral—even as it is today.

However, after undergoing extensive renovation at the same time the Arch was being built, it was declared a basilica in 1961 by Pope John XXIII and is now one of the city's principal tourist attractions, as well as a fashionable church for Catholic weddings.

The Greek Revival Fashion

In the late 1820's the citizens of the United States likened our successful fight for independence from England with the war then going on between Greece and Turkey as the former struggled to free itself from Turkish rule. Everything Greek became the rage in the wake of this popular cause. And a wave of Greek Revival architecture swept the land which included designs for buildings of every type and use from necessary houses (outdoor privies) to elaborate homes, small domiciles, imposing churches, banks and other structures of a grand scale.

The four-winged Old Courthouse, begun in 1839, is another of the city's Greek Revival treasures. The Italian Renaissance dome, which replaced a less imposing cupola, was added in 1863 when that style had become the fashion.

Land for a courthouse for Saint Louis County (the City of Saint Louis was a part of Saint Louis County until 1876) was given by Auguste Chouteau, a founder of Saint Louis, and Judge James B. Lucas, another prominent citizen and large landowner who had come here in 1805 when appointed by President Jefferson to help settle the Spanish Land Grant claims. This gift to the county was given with the stipulation that if the building erected on it should not be used as a courthouse, the land was to revert to their respective heirs. In 1933 when the new Civil Courts Building was finished and put into use, a lengthy law suit followed with the Lucas and Chouteau heirs trying to regain possession of this now immensely valuable piece of property. The suit, which went all the way to the U.S. Supreme Court, was finally settled in favor of the People of Saint Louis. The building, now owned and maintained by the National Park Service, is another of the city's prime tourist attractions.

Chatillon-DeMenil Mansion
3352 DeMenil Place.
Originally built in 1848 as a simple farm house by Henri Chatillon, intrepid guide for Francis Parkman on the latter's famous Western trip. An important result of this trip was Parkman's book, THE OREGON TRAIL, which was highly influential in helping to spark the western migration movement.

In 1857 the house and the then much more extensive grounds were purchased by Dr. Nicholas DeMenil and his partners, with the idea of using the underground caves that honeycomb this section for the beer storage of their newly formed brewery.

When the brewery was not a success, DeMenil bought out his partners to use the estate for his family's summer place. During the Civil War, the DeMenils, ardent Confederate sympathizers, moved here on a year-around basis to escape harassments from Union forces. Thus, it was not until 1863 — long after the craze for the Greek Revival style had waned — that the elaborate Ionic portico and iron work were added in an extensive remodeling of the house.

Restored by Landmarks, Inc., it is now a museum that tells a lively story of early Saint Louis.

Some of the most pleasingly graceful historic houses that have survived in the Saint Louis metroplex—and all of them true treasures—are Greek Revival architecture.

Martin Hanley Esq. House, (1854)
7600 Westmoreland Avenue
Clayton.
Built for his family after Hanley's return from the California gold fields. Typical of the plantation houses so prevalent in Southern States before the Civil War, today this style epitomizes the ante-bellum South.

Restored by the City of Clayton, the Hanley House is the only pre-Civil War domicile in Clayton and one of the few in the nation to be completely restored with its original furnishings. It is also a monument of sorts to the deep division of feelings that existed between family, friends and neighbors during the War Between the States, for many tales have been passed down about the house and the Hanley family (strongly Southern in their loyalties), their struggles and hardships during this conflict.

Now open to the public, the house is owned and maintained by the City of Clayton.

John B. Meyers House (1869)
180 Dunn Road.
Overlooking Highway I-270 in Florissant, this house was saved from demolition only after a long and bitter confrontation between Historic Florissant, Inc., and the Missouri State Highway Department. Its preservation marked a precedent-setting case when the house was officially recognized as a landmark of the City of Florissant by the Federal Department of Transportation. This prevented its destruction. It is now occupied by various art, craft and antique shops.

Fishback House, (1858)
440 East Argonne Avenue.
One of the oldest buildings in Kirkwood and considered a good example of Greek Revival architecture although the house shows some of the Victorian influences then coming to the fore.

Judge Wilson Primm's Law Office (1850's)
313 Iron Street, Carondelet.
Primm, one of Saint Louis' most prominent nineteenth-century citizens as well as the descendent of several of the original French families, fled Saint Louis in 1849 with his family when the disastrous fire of that year destroyed his home and his son nearly perished in the cholera epidemic. He built a new home in Carondelet and re-established his flourishing law practice there.

Primm was the keynote speaker at the ceremony for the laying of the corner stone of the Old Courthouse, October 29, 1839.

All three of these excellent examples of the Doric, Ionic and Corinthian Orders can be seen from the same vantage point.

Holy Corners

In the earlier years of this century when a solid Greek classical education was considered the hallmark of every well-educated person, parents would often take their offspring to "Holy Corners" (Kingshighway at Washington Avenue) to enable them to get the Greek Orders straight in their thinking. (Still good for this purpose.) For here are excellent examples of each of the orders: Corinthian (former Temple Israel, now Angelic Temple of Deliverance); Ionic, Saint John's Methodist Church; and Doric (very similar to the Romans' Tuscan Order), Tuscan Masonic Lodge.

Saint John's Methodist Church
Architect: Theodore Link.

Former Temple Israel, now Angelic Temple of
Deliverance
Architects: Eames and Young.

Tuscan Masonic Lodge
Architect: Albert B. Groves.

Oakland (1850)
7820 Genesta Avenue, Affton
Architect: George I. Barnett.
Built for wealthy Saint Louis banker, Louis Benoist, as the country home for his large family (thirteen living children), it is now considered one of the Midwest's best remaining Italianate villas.

A well-known national personage to spend a good part of his childhood at Oakland was Condé Nast, one of Benoist's many grandchildren. Nast, founder of both Vogue and Vanity Fair magazines, was one of the most influential publishers of his time (1920's and '30's).

Restored by the Affton Historical Society, Oakland has excellent community support and—like the days of old—it is now the center of a never-ending series of events (parties of various kinds, celebrations, tours, meetings, etc.).

The Italianate Style

Next to follow in architectural fashion across the United States after the Greek Revival style had run its course was the Italianate villa, patterned after the architecture of the Italian Renaissance period. This style first became popular in England when Queen Victoria and Prince Albert built their new home, "Osbourne House," in this imposing fashion on the Isle of Wight in 1848. Now, instead of the stately pillars topped by graceful capitals reminiscent of a Greek temple, everyone who could afford it wanted an Italianate-towered home instead. "So romantic looking!" was the general consensus.

Superintendent's House (1868)
Tower Grove Park
Architect: Francis Tunica.
Another good example of Italianate architecture, this house was built by Henry Shaw for James Gurney, Superintendent of Tower Grove Park whom Shaw brought to Saint Louis from the Royal Botanical Gardens in England. Gurney and Shaw designed the park as a Victorian walking garden, which it essentially remains.
Still used as the park superintendent's home.

Dr. Franz Arzt House (1878)
2322 South Twelfth Street.
A delightful mixture of the Italianate villa-towered style and the mansard roof which has become the insignia of the Victorian Age, Arzt's house was the last word in modernity when it was built. A hot-water heating system (the second in Saint Louis); a system of flues and ceiling vents to keep the house cool in the summer; and the first private greenhouse in the city.

A highly respected South Side physician, Arzt was also celebrated for his night-blooming cereuses and people came from all over the city to view them (entertainment offerings were not nearly so numerous then as today). And, although there are many caves in this part of Saint Louis, Arzt's home had none, so the good doctor built his own, complete with stalactites and stalagmites imported from all over the world.

Typical small dwelling from the latter part of the nineteenth century. Many similar ones remain in the older sections of the city. Some have true mansard roofs; some have just the front so decorated, as in this example.

French
Second Empire Architecture
(Victorian)

Close on the heels of the Italianate style of architecture came the French Second Empire. With a graceful mansard roof (named for Francois Mansard, the seventeenth-century architect who first designed it), this roof line had been revived and became all the rage in France during the years of the Second Empire (1853-1870), hence its name. Soon adopted in the United States for almost every type of building (and this was a period of tremendous building activity across the land), it has come to be known generally in this country as the Victorian style.

With an appealing charm and suitable for both imposing mansions as well as small dwellings, examples are plentiful in all of the older sections of Saint Louis.

Blair-Huse Mansion
2043 Park Avenue.
The nucleus of this house was built in the 1850's for Montgomery Blair, Postmaster General in Lincoln's first-term cabinet. In 1878 the property was purchased by William Huse who engaged George I. Barnett to modernize the dwelling and enlarge it by adding the present front section so that it faced Park Avenue instead of Benton Place as formerly.

With the decline of Lafayette Park as a fashionable residential section after the 1896 cyclone, this house, woefully neglected, became a dilapidated rooming house accommodating over fifty people. Its restoration and rehabilitation in the late 1960's and early 1970's back to its former elegance, was a key factor in the revitalization of the now "so-chic" Lafayette Park area. For the subsequent publicity of his heroic efforts given to twenty-two year old Timothy Conley who undertook the task, opened the eyes of others to the architectural treasures that abound in the square and streets around the park.

A recent fire gutted the interior but it has been restored once again. It remains one of Saint Louis' best examples of this hand-some style.

2631 South Twelfth Street.
Built in 1873 for Louis Obert, founder and owner of the Arsenal Brewery, one of
the many prosperous nineteenth-century local breweries.

Typical dwellings of prosperous South Side Germans (circa 1870).

The Germans

Gottfried Duden of Germany came into this area in 1824, did a little farming at Dutzow in nearby Warren County and then returned to his homeland in 1829 where, at his own expense, he published *Report About A Journey to the Western States of North America.* This book, which pictured Missouri as a utopian paradise, immediately became a best seller.

Conditions in Germany—social, political and economic—were ripe with discontent at this time. Because of these myriad difficulties, many were voluntarily leaving *der vaterland;* others, caught up in the revolutions of 1839 and 1849, fled for their lives. Missouri, described so glowingly in Duden's book, seemed a perfect refuge.

Thousands of these Germans came to Saint Louis during the period beginning in the mid-1830's and extending to the final years of the century. They took over North and South Saint Louis which became German cities within the city. Although other ethnic groups came here from Europe during this time, none came in such numbers. None influenced the development of the city so much. None left such a mark on the architecture of the city. And the homes that housed these enterprising, hard-working, music-loving, beer-enjoying (as well as often highly educated) groups still line the streets of their former special sections of Saint Louis to tell their story for many years to come.

1812 South Eighth Street (1850's).
Half-flounder house (so-called because the roof line supposedly resembled the head of the flounder fish) was a popular style with Saint Louis Germans. For, as the house was theoretically only half-finished, taxes were correspondingly lower.

1631 Missouri Avenue.
Many financially successful Saint Louis Germans soon developed a taste for much more elaborate houses than the severely plain ones of the earlier generations of local Germans.

Architect Ernst Janssen's ornate, rococo style was especially liked by them. A number of the houses (usually unmistakable) that Janssen designed are to be found in the South Side residential sections where these prosperous Germans lived.

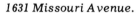

Statue of Friedrich Schiller
Sculptor: Ernest Rau.
Originally in Rauschenbach Park, North Saint Louis, another section once favored by well-to-do Germans. Now on Market Street Mall.

An exact reproduction of the Schiller statue in Marbach, Germany, the poet's birthplace, this statue was a gift to beautify the park in the 1890's by Schiller admirers.

Samuel Cupples House (1890)

3673 West Pine Boulevard
Architect: Thomas Annan.

Presently on the campus of Saint Louis University and although twice it narrowly missed the headache ball, the Cupples House is now elegantly restored and open to the public as a museum. It is also in constant use for social, civic and educational functions. Its art gallery serves as the main gallery for the university's art collection as well as having a continual series of art exhibitions. With its glimpses of the past extravagances of the rich and an excellent example of the Richardson style and a way of life that has gone with the wind, the house adds another dimension to Saint Louis life.

In the U.S. industrial expansion that followed in the wake of the Civil War, immense fortunes were made. And most of these new millionaires soon built large, imposing mansions as testimonies to their wealth.

Favored nation-wide by many of them was the Romanesque, looking-like-a-fortress style. Named the Richardson Style for Henry Hobbs Richardson, the talented Boston architect who developed it in this country, its grim solidness seemed to say something important to these new rich for this type of house swept the land. The Samuel Cupples House completed in 1890—and with money no object—is considered one of the best surviving examples in the U.S.

Cupples made his fortune in the wooden ware business and the Cupples Stations, a series of warehouses built near the railroads which greatly facilitated the handling of freight coming into or going out of Saint Louis. These warehouses played a vital role in helping to make this city a thriving manufacturing center. A generous philanthropist, Cupples gave the bulk of his fortune to civic endeavors. His gift to Washington University of the Cupples Stations formed a significant part of that school's endowment for many years. Among other generous gifts, he gave two buildings to Washington University (which continue to bear his name); the land for Barnes Hospital; and founded an orphanage.

Illustrated on this page is but a small sample of the stone carvings that decorate the exterior of the Cupples House. Stone artisans were imported from England for this purpose; it is believed that their own faces were used for the stone portraits.

Kingsbury Place Gates

The Private Place

Private Places, the unique contribution made by Saint Louis to urban living, have played a critical role in the development of the city, as well as maintaining the stability of their neighborhoods. Private Places are characterized by the streets being closed to public traffic so that quiet and privacy might be assured (this is possible because the ownership and maintenance of the streets is by the residents); and strict deed restrictions (no roomers, no boarders, no commercial enterprises, proper lawn care, etc.) enforced through an association in each private place to which all residents must belong.

All Private Places have entrance gates, often very handsome, which contribute to the feeling of being isolated from the busy world and almost all also have a carefully tended parkstrip which helps to simulate the feeling of country living. So successful was this concept, especially in the latter years of the nineteenth century and the early part of the present, that living in a Private Place became the way of life for most wealthy Saint Louisans.

As a consequence many of the city's most expensive and beautiful houses were built in these Private Places. Most were developed at a time when it was fashionable to look to past civilizations for architectural inspiration. Thus, Egyptian temples, Greek temples, Italian palazzos, French Renaissance chateaus, French palaces, Tudor manor houses, Romanesque, Georgian, American colonial styles are all here—and in fairly close proximity. Indeed a tour of the various Private Places can best be likened to a good course in Western World architecture.

French Renaissance Chateau (1898)
13 Portland Place
Architect: W. Albert Swazey.
Built for William Bixby, wealthy philanthropist, art patron and civic leader.

Egyptian Temple (1909)
27 Washington Terrace
Architects: Barnett, Haynes and Barnett.
Built for Dr. Robert O'Reilly, prominent physician.

Italian Renaissance Palazzo (1898),
23 Portland Place
Architects: Eames and Young.
Built for William McMillan, president of the Missouri Car and Foundry Company (later the American Car and Foundry Company).

34 Benton Place (1871)
Architect: Probably John H. Maurice
Built for Judge and Mrs. James Lindley.
  Benton Place, the first Private Place in Saint Louis, was platted in 1866 by Julius Pitzman for Montgomery Blair, prominent national politician and brother of Frank P. Blair, Jr. (see page 94).
  Pitzman was eventually to plat all of the major Private Places in Saint Louis.
  Once a stylish neighborhood, Benton Place, a victim of urban growth, became shabby and rundown. Now, almost completely restored, its houses awash with Victorian charm, it is another Saint Louis prize show place.

Doorways

An especially delightful bequest from Saint Louis' golden age of domestic architecture (1866-1916) are the handsome doorways. For there is an overwhelming wealth of stunning entrance ways from this period gracing the city. These examples are but a few of the many.

53 Westmoreland Place (1908)
Architect: James Jamieson
Built for L. Freund.

15 Kingsbury Place (1905)
Architect: George Hellmuth
Built for Sidney Blackwell.

3505 Hawthorne Boulevard (1895)
Compton Heights
Architect: Ernst Janssen
Built for Charles Dieckriede.

325 Westgate (1914)
Parkview Place
Architect: Not known
Built for Walter Johnson.

2115 Park Avenue (1869)
Architect: George I. Barnett.
Built for George Bain, flour merchant,
president of the Merchant's Exchange.

5145 Lindell Boulevard (1899)
Architects: Eames and Young.
Built for Mr. and Mrs. E.P. Graham. Mrs.
Graham was the daughter of Frank Blair, Jr.,
Missouri Civil War hero.

Her mother (Blair's widow) also lived
(and died) here with her valiant husband's
public statue but a stone's throw away.

Doorway modeled after the famous one at
Westover House in Virginia, considered the
most beautiful of all the Tidewater plantations.

Eleven Kingsbury Place (1902)
Architects: Barnett, Haynes and Barnett.
Second oldest house in Kingsbury Place; built
for the Henry Elliots. Their daughter
Elizabeth married Edward Mallinckrodt, Jr.
whose father founded the Mallinckrodt
Chemical Company.

One Westmoreland Place (1895)
Architect: W. Albert Swazey.
Built for Jacob Van Blarcom, banker. His
wife, an avid hostess, famous for her Sunday
Night Open Houses, was the first woman in
Saint Louis to require a social secretary.

3263 Hawthorne Place (1895)
Architect: Ernst Janssen.
Home of Louis Stockstrom, co-inventor of the gas cooking range (one of the foremost liberators of womankind) and co-founder of the Quick Meal Stove company.

5045 Lindell Boulevard (1902)
Architect: W. Albert Swazey
Built for Mr. and Mrs. James Green and Mr. and Mrs. Walter Thompson.
Legend has it that the house was built by the two families to accommodate relatives and friends visiting the 1904 World's Fair. Later, it served as the family home of the Thompsons for many years.

Two Hortense Place (1904)
Architect: George Hellmuth.
Home of Albert Bond Lambert of the Lambert Pharmacal Company (Listerine); backer of Lindbergh's 1927 Overseas Flight to Paris. Lambert Saint Louis International Airport is named in his honor.

One Portland Place (1911)
Architect: Tom Barnett.
Built for the Edward Fausts. Mrs. Faust was the daughter of Adolphus Busch; Mr. Faust was the son of Tony Faust, renowned restauranteur.

Elaborate entrance gate.

Statue of stag at entrance to estate.
In the parkland of Grant's Farm, there are a number of live stags with equally impressive antlers.

Grant's Farm

A resplendent exception to the Saint Louis "turn-of-the-century very rich living in Private Places" syndrome is the Adolphus Busch estate with its Gothic castle situated on Gravois Road.

In spite of his great wealth and many civic philanthropies, Adolphus Busch and his family were not accepted by Saint Louis' rigid, snobbish social establishment because of his beer connection. And this was an era when Society (with a large capital S) was all-important, especially to the women of a family. For in spite of their riches, there were few outlets for socially prominent women except to entertain or be entertained.

Busch went his own way. He built a romantic castle reminiscent of the Rhine River castles of his homeland; elaborate stables for his fine horses (forerunners of the Busch Brewery's now world-famous Clydesdales); stocked his grounds with exotic animals and birds; founded his own country club (Sunset Hills) and his own restaurant (Bevo Mill).

The estate, named Grant's Farm because of the Ulysses S. Grant restored log cabin on the grounds, is presently owned by Busch's equally philanthropic and colorful grandson, August A. Busch, Jr. A large part of the parklands is open to the public and good times and happy memories have been provided for the thousands who have enjoyed its zoo, train rides through the grounds and free beer served to visitors in the Bauernhoff.

The Busch Castle (1911)
Architects: Widman and Walsh.

Log cabin, built in 1856 by Ulysses S. Grant for his family after he had resigned his army commission and returned from the West to try to make a living as a farmer. The house was named ''Hardscrabble'' because of the difficult times the Grants underwent during this period.

During the 1904 Saint Louis World's Fair, the cabin was used for the Blanke Coffee Exhibit. At the Fair's conclusion, Adolphus Busch purchased the cabin, moved it to this location (not too far from its original site on South Rock Hill Road) and named the impressive estate in its honor. The cabin, recently restored, is open to the public for a glimpse of how the Grants lived during their occupancy of it.

Masonic Temple
3681 Lindell Boulevard
Architect: Albert B. Grove.
In ancient times temples for worship were usually built on a high cliff or natural rock elevation; the best known of all such existing temples is the Parthenon on the Acropolis in Greece.
The impressive Masonic Temple, dedicated in 1926, and built in three steps to symbolize the three steps in Freemasonry, is modeled after it and is considered one of the great buildings in the United States from this era of looking backwards to older civilizations for architectural inspiration.

Architectural Influences From The Past

The philosophy that beautiful buildings helped to make better citizens, so prevalent in the latter years of the nineteenth century and early years of the twentieth, had a forceful impact on buildings all across the nation. For, following this line of thought, many buildings erected during this period—public, private and domestic—were copies of - or inspired by - great buildings from other periods of history.

Some of the most noteworthy buildings in Saint Louis are the result of this philosophic idea. All add immeasureably to the beauty of the city. But whether they contributed to a more upstanding citizenry will forever be one of those intangible unknowns.

Altar and reredoes, the crowning glory of Christ Church Episcopal Cathedral, are modeled after the fifteenth-century, high altar screens of England's Saint Alban's Abbey and Winchester Cathedral. All are fashioned from Caen stone from ancient quarries in Normandy, the same stone used to build most of the medieval Gothis churches of Europe.

Sculptor: Harry Helms of Exeter, England, who was also responsible for replacing the statues of the reredoes of Saint Alban's and Winchester Cathedral which had been destroyed almost three-hundred years earlier by Cromwell's Army.

Gift of Mrs. Christine Graham.

Brookings Hall
Washington University.
Modeled after Windsor Castle, England, (built in medieval times), it is named for Robert Brookings, president of the university (1897-1914) and a key figure in moving the school to this location. The building was finished in time to be used as the Administration Building of the 1904 Saint Louis World's Fair.

Architects: The Cope and Stewardson Firm of Philadelphia who won the nationwide competition in 1899 to design the buildings for the new campus of Washington University to be near Forest Park. Their firm included the prime architects of the Collegiate Gothic style, then in high favor for the many new college buildings being erected across the land. (The buildings at Princeton University and Bryn Mawr College of this period are other examples of their work.)

Graham Chapel, Washington University. Inspired by the fifteenth-century King's Chapel, Cambridge University, England, considered one of the most beautiful buildings in the world.

Architectural firm: Cope and Stewardson but after the design of James Jamison, who came here from Philadelphia to oversee the construction of the Cope and Stewardson competition-winning buildings. Jamison eventually moved to Saint Louis and established his own architectural firm which became responsible for some of the city's finest buildings.

Gift of Mrs. Christine Graham.

Stone gargoyle decorating door frame.

Door to chapel. Note carved stone heads.

One of the numerous figures, all expressing various human emotions, that adorn the richly carved interior wooden dais screen.

Civil Courts Building (1932)
Tucker Boulevard and Market Street
Architects: Klipstein and Rathmann.
    Classic temple atop is replica of the tomb of King Mausolus built in 342 B.C. at Halicarnassus in Asia Minor, one of the seven wonders of the Ancient World. However, at the apex two sphinx-like figures have been substituted for the original statuary of a four-horse chariot driven by King Mausolus.

South Entrance (1912), Soulard Market
Architect: Albert Osburg.
Inspired by Brunelleschi's Foundling Hospital, Florence,
Italy (1419), the first true Renaissance building.

Urn
One Portland Place.
A copy of the famous Warwick Vase found in the
late 1700's in the 2000-year old ruins of Hadrian's
Villa at Tivoli outside Rome; owned by the Earls of
Warwick for two centuries, it was sold to meet
death duties by the present heir and is now in the
British Museum.

Linnean House (1882)
Missouri Botanical Garden.
One of the oldest greenhouses
still in use in U.S.
Architect: George I. Barnett.
Modeled after the Orangery,
Kensington Gardens,
England, so-named as its
original purpose was to
protect orange trees, first
imported from Spain in the
seventeenth century, from
the rigors of English winters.

47

Carved wooden corbel, typical of a German Gothic church.
As all art in the Middle Ages was of a religious nature, artistic talent found many odd expressions, such as the grotesque corbels found in many medieval churches.

Saint Francis de Sales Church
Ohio Avenue at Gravois.
Begun in the 1890's, completed in 1908. Designed to be the cathedral for German-speaking Saint Louis Catholics, Saint Francis de Sales Church, whose steeple is the city's tallest, is typical of the Gothic, single-spired churches, so commonplace in Germany.

   Although its exterior was planned to be a copy of Saint Paul's in Berlin (two spires), financial difficulties forced the congregation to settle for one spire, so the church ended up being very similar to the renowned Ulm Cathedral instead.

Interior of Saint Francis de Sales Church.
The ornate, carved, wooden, Gothic-style altar is a copy of Saint Paul's Cathedral, Berlin.

Saint Francis Xavier Church (1897)
(College Church)
Grand Avenue at Lindell Boulevard.
Established and maintained by the Jesuits of Saint Louis University. The present structure, which dates from the 1890's, is patterned after Saint Colman's Cathedral, Cobh, Ireland, designed by the noted English architect, A. Pugin, celebrated for his role in the nineteenth-century Gothic revival movement, and architect of the English Parliament Buildings.

Saint John the Apostle and Evangelist Church (1860)
15 Plaza Square.
Built at the time that the Italiante style was at its peak in this country, the design of Saint John's tower was heavily influenced by the famous Renaissance towers of fifteenth-century Italy.

Saint Louis Union Station

The restoration of the medieval walled city of Carcassonne in the south of France in the nineteenth century won international accolades. As much of the original fortress was built under the direction of King Louis IX, what better inspiration for the new Saint Louis Union Station? Especially as this was a time when there was a nostalgic looking backwards to the city's French heritage.

The building of the station was begun in July, 1893; opened with jubilant fanfare on September 1, 1894; and for many years was one of the busiest railroad hubs in the nation. Thousands passed through its doors each day. But with the dwindling of railroad traffic, the crowds grew ever smaller. And non-existent when Amtrak moved to other quarters.

Empty and forlorn looking, the old station stood for several years, a massive obsolescent, stone hulk. A few attempts were made to find uses for it and the immense train shed. All failed. Until 1981. In that year another group of investors—mostly from outside of the city—combined to raise the necessary capital for a complete restoration of the station complex to its pristine glory with an elegant hotel and an unusual shopping mall. After all, what other shopping mall has the bastions (even if just copies) of an ancient walled city for its facade!

Example of some of the elaborate plaster and gilt work that decorates the former Great Hall of the Union Station, now the lounge of the Omni International Hotel.

On August 29, 1985, the Saint Louis Union Station enjoyed a second gala opening in its honor. Marching bands, entertainment of various sorts, dignitaries from everywhere, laudatory speeches and a huge crowd in a carnival spirit celebrated the occasion, another of the city's golden moments.

1894 Architect: Theodore Link
Restoration Architects: Hellmuth, Obata and Kassabaum.

One of the iron lamps that graces the entranceway.

Tiffany stained glass window in the former Great Hall symbolizes the unification of the nation from coast to coast by railroads. The figure in the middle represents Saint Louis; the one on the east (right side), New York; the one on the west, San Francisco.

Saint Louis Public Library

One of the city's most magnificent buildings, and another direct result of the philosophy that great architecture makes for better citizens, is the Saint Louis Public Library at Thirteenth and Olive Streets.

Erected on the site of one-time Indian camping grounds, this splendid example of the Italian Renaissance palazzo style was dedicated in 1913. It was hailed nationally at that time as one of the country's most important public buildings of the past quarter of a century.

Architect: Cass Gilbert.

Mosaic of Saint Michael the Archangel by Volpon (1859); inspired by the famous Guido Reni painting, Cappaccini Church, Rome.
Location: Hallway, main floor of library.

Detail of flagpole, a copy of the flagpoles that decorate Saint Mark's Square, Venice.

Exterior and interior lamp standards.

Both the exterior and the interior of the library have many architectural details of unusual beauty that are deserving of far more appreciation than they are customarily accorded. Here are but a few.

THE LOVE OF LEARNING, THE
SEQUESTERED NOOKS,
AND ALL THE SWEET SERENITY
OF BOOKS. HENRY W. LONGFELLOW.

Italian Renaissance-styled fountain with Victorian epigram.

Kilpatrick-Ross house (1914)
33 Portland Place
Architect: E.P. Russell.
A miniature palace inspired by the Petit Trianon at Versailles, a special favorite of Marie Antoinette's and one of the triumphs of French architecture.

The house was built for Mr. and Mrs. Claude Kilpatrick. Mrs. Kilpatrick was the daughter of John Liggett, one of the founders of the Liggett and Meyers Tobacco Company.

Present Owner: Mrs. Gladney Ross, daughter of Frank Gladney, one of the founders of the Seven-Up Company.

Henry Shaw Town House (1850)
2311 Tower Grove Boulevard
Architect: George I. Barnett.
Another jewel in Saint Louis' rich architectural heritage inspired by great buildings from earlier civilizations is the Henry Shaw Town House. Patterned after the Laradeli family's Renaissance palace in Florence, Italy, which Shaw no doubt saw and admired on his European travels.

Following the directive in Shaw's will, the house was moved, brick by brick, from a site on the southwest corner of Seventh and Locust Streets to the Missouri Botanical Garden. This unquestionably saved it from being demolished in the city's westward commercial expansion and thus it is one of a very small number of remaining ante-bellum mansions built for wealthy personages of that era. Now used for administration purposes at the Garden.

650 East Monroe Avenue
Kirkwood
Architect: Harris Armstrong.
Built in 1939 for a homesick family transplanted from Virginia, this house was once declared by ''House and Garden Magazine'' as the most authentic of its type outside of Williamsburg.
*   Architect Armstrong is best known for his contemporary architectural work. But at the beginning of his distinguished career and before designing the above house, his clients sent him to Williamsburg to imbibe the spirit of that eighteenth-century capital.*

Zoo Wall
Architect: William Bernoudy.
Inspired by the serpentine wall at the University of Virginia designed by Thomas Jefferson.

An anomaly, the Armbruster Mortuary on Clayton Road is a copy of a Scottish Highland castle that was torn down, transported to Des Moines, Iowa, and re-erected there.
*   The interior large room, used for the chapel and funeral services, with its soaring ceiling, enormous stone fireplace, oak paneling and a musicians' gallery, is typical of the grand baronial halls found in medieval Scottish and English castles.*
*   Pictured is an entrance to the castle stronghold.*

One of the lions decorating the steps of the present City Hall of University City
Sculptor: William Bailey.
The lion, a symbol of power since ancient times, was adopted by Lewis as his totem and he used lions in every conceivable fashion to embellish his new city. Recently the Administration of University City adopted a stylized version of a lion and lioness as the city's logo in recognition of Lewis' many vital contributions to University City and what it became.

Lewis's Magazine Building, built 1903
Headquarters for Lewis' publishing empire
Architect: Herbert Chivers, whom Lewis first sent to Europe for architectural inspiration.
Now the City Hall for University City, it was chosen by the Smithsonian Institution in 1984 as one of the most outstanding city halls of the nation and was part of its nation-wide exhibit on this subject.

University City

Almost all of the suburbs surrounding the city of Saint Louis have interesting beginnings. Florissant and Carondelet were French settlements of about the same vintage as Saint Louis. Webster Groves and Kirkwood came into being as a result of the new railroads running West which made access to the city proper both convenient and reasonable. Clayton owes its origin to being chosen as the county seat when the City of Saint Louis withdrew from Saint Louis County in 1876. And so it goes. Each community has its own story to tell. But none has as colorful and flamboyant beginnings as University City, the result of one man's dream.

Edward Gardner Lewis, magazine publisher, founded University City in the early 1900's as the center of his publishing empire. He incorporated it, became its mayor in 1906 and its chief developer. Dreaming ever larger dreams, he planned for his People's University to become a national major art and intellectual center; his People's Bank a financial center (Lewis invented banking by mail); and the American Women's League which he also founded was to make University City the capital of the women's liberation movement. Lewis truly was a man far ahead of his time.

Stairway, former Magazine Building, now City Hall for University City.

Art Institute of the People's University, 1909
Architects: Eames and Young.
As part of his plan to make University City the center of the ceramic world, Lewis engaged Taxile Doat of France, a world-renowned ceramicist, to be the head of the Ceramic Department of the People's University. Some of the glazes subsequently developed here won wide recognition.

After the failure of the university, the building was used for a variety of purposes. Now it has come full circle with parts of it being used to provide additional studio room for the Washington University School of Fine Arts.

But Lewis' dreams were far too big; and he stepped on too many Establishment toes. Then, depending on whose side one is on, he was either mercilessly persecuted by government forces (generally accepted today) or really a first-class con man. Although the government brought three separate trials against him, it was never able to obtain a verdict proving him guilty of anything. But it was able to cancel his mailing privileges so that Lewis could not continue his publishing ventures (at one time almost one-fourth of the mail exiting from Saint Louis was his publications). This edict forced him into bankruptcy; and in 1912 he left University City for California. But he left behind a rich legacy in the city that he and his wife Mabel founded.

Ornate plaster identification insignia of the Lewis Publishing Company on his former Press Building, now one of the municipal buildings for University City.
Note lion heads on stringcourse.

Lioness, female of the pair on the pillars of the University City Gates, entrance to Lewis' "City Beautiful"
Sculptor: George Zolnay.

Thirteen-hundred block, South Tenth Street.

The Brick City

After the disastrous fire of 1849 which destroyed so much of the old town, an ordinance was passed requiring that all future buildings be of either stone or brick. As this was a period of burgeoning growth for Saint Louis and many buildings for various uses were necessary to fulfill the needs of this expansion, and as brick was the cheaper material, a number of brick works were quickly established. And the streets of Saint Louis were soon lined with new brick structures. Big, little and in-between. Some ugly, some handsome, some nondescript. But all of brick. Small wonder that Saint Louis became known as "the brick city."

Eighteen-hundred block Lafayette Boulevard.

*905 Morrison Street.
Another well-restored house in the LaSalle-Park
Redevelopment Project.*

*Saint John Nepomuk Church (first Czechoslovakian
church in the U.S.)
Eleventh Street and Lafayette Boulevard.*

Single dwellings, adjoining town houses, flats, churches, business buildings—there are literally hundreds of examples of this late nineteenth and early twentieth century brick work to be found in both North and South Saint Louis. It is now being referred to by architectural authorities as "a national architectural treasure."

*Street in North Saint Louis. Its duplication can be
found in all of the older parts of the city.*

*North Saint Louis has not fared quite so well in
its rehabilitation as South Saint Louis but a
movement there is now beginning to get un-
derway.
It, too, has wonderful possibilities that,
restored, can be counted among the city's brick
architectural heritage.*

2018 Lafayette Avenue.

Architectural Embellishments

To relieve the monotony of the severely plain facades of the brick houses and other buildings that were going up as rapidly as possible to accommodate the city's growing population during this period, elaborate cornices, decorative doorways and window lintels, iron balconies and fences were widely used. Many examples remain to enhance the city.

911 Park Avenue.

912 and 916 Hickory Street.

922 - 26 - 28 Morrison Street.

The houses on this page are in the LaSalle-Park Redevelopment Project.

915 Morrison Street.

Fence, Lafayette Park.
Established in 1836, Lafayette Park was the first public park in Saint Louis and the first park west of the Mississippi River.

When the fence was erected in the late 1860's to enclose the park, an enormous ruckus was generated over spending so much money for it. Today, its old-fashioned, nostalgic charm from another age continues to give pleasure to many who enjoy the park - and to passersby.

Decorative Iron

Because of the iron mines only a few miles south of Saint Louis and the excellent transportation from there (the Iron Mountain Railroad) along with the fashion of the times, numerous iron foundries (over forty)—and whose fame for their fine craftsmanship spread throughout the country—flourished here until well into the twentieth century.

Even today, although a great deal of this decorative iron has been destroyed or purchased by antique dealers from other cities, Saint Louis continues to be blessed with an inordinate amount of their graceful work.

Balconies, balconies, balconies...

916 Hickory Street (1859).
Iron porch formerly on front of house, moved to side location by John Rodabaugh, first new settler (1977) in the LaSalle-Park Redevelopment Project. When he moved in, there was no electricity, plumbing or water.

The project, which comprises 137 acres just south of the World Headquarters of the Ralston Purina Company, and one of the most ambitious urban renewal programs undertaken anywhere in the United States, was accomplished by Ralston Purina and the Saint Louis Land Clearance Authority.

Their efforts - and lots of money - converted a badly deteriorated slum, forsaken by everyone except a few desparately poor, into another Saint Louis show place. Tours of this area are now high on the list of things to do in Saint Louis.

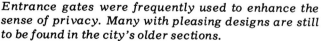

Iron fence, restored house
921 Park Avenue.

Entrance gates were frequently used to enhance the sense of privacy. Many with pleasing designs are still to be found in the city's older sections.

63

Iron railing, DeMenil Mansion's back veranda.

Section of Old Courthouse fence commemorating a pet turtle that lived in the courthouse fountain base for a number of years and a frequent subject of newspaper quips.

Detail of Tower Grove Park fence.

Portland Place Gate.

3406 Hawthorne Place.

Washington Terrace Entrance Gate.

*B'Nai Amoona Cemetery
800 block of Blackberry Avenue, University City.*

21 Washington Terrace.

Pre-contemporary architecture in Saint Louis continued to develop a wealth of ornamentation. Statues, gargoyles, caryatids, scroll work, bas reliefs, high reliefs, fancy ballustrades — so many objects to please the eye and fire the imagination.

Stone, brick work, iron, terra cotta were all used to create these embellishments which give to these buildings from yesterday an interesting *joie de vivre* that the buildings of today are unable to convey.

Saint Michael and Saint George Episcopal Church, Clayton.

Saint Louis City Art Museum North Facade.

Jefferson Memorial Building West Wall.

Former Mississippi Valley Trust
Building. Now Lerwick Medical
Clinic
Fourth & Pine Streets.

American Theater
416 North Ninth Street.

Hadley Square
Building
1101 Lucas Avenue.

911 Washington Avenue (formerly Lammerts Furniture Store).

Architects: Eames and Young.

Built in 1898 for the Lammert Furniture Company. Founded in 1861 by Martin Lammert, sixteen-year old German immigrant, the Lammert Furniture Store became the largest (ten-stories) and most prestigious store of its kind in this part of the Midwest. But with changing times and the move to outlying shopping centers such a big downtown store, no longer practical, was closed.

The building, empty and abandoned for several years, was purchased by the Pantheon Company, local leader in the rehabilitation of old, sound but dilapidated buildings, to be made into offices and other commercial enterprises.

Detail of the elaborate capitals.

Caryatid
Entrance, Famous Barr Downtown Store.

Wainwright Building (1891)
Architect: Louis Sullivan.
Note varied terra cotta decorations at each window level.

Dragon motif balustrade
3505 Longfellow Boulevard.

Stone wall
One Portland Place.

The traditional mythological figures that adorn the cupola of the Old Post Office are typical of the taste of the time. They are noteworthy amongst the treasures of the city primarily because of being the work of Daniel Chester French (his second commission), who became the dean of American sculptors in the early years of the twentieth century.

Old Post Office (formerly the U.S. Custom House), 1874
Architect: A. Mullett.

Erected in the troubled post-Civil War years, the former Custom House was built to be a fortress. A thirty-foot surrounding moat; windows with sliding iron shutters and holes for rifle barrels; and a well in the basement to provide water in case of attack, it was a stronghold to withstand any siege.

The building was saved from demolition in the 1970's after more than a decade of long, hard fighting between local preservation groups and the "tear-down-all-old-buildings" school. Now restored, with the three upper floors used for government offices and the lower floors for commercial ventures, this massively solid Second Empire structure forms an integral link of continuity between the architecture of old Saint Louis and the new Saint Louis.

Tony, the Vegetable Man
Atop Antonio's Produce Market
South Seventh Street and Lafayette
Avenue.
An old-time street vendor of fruits
and vegetables, said to be modeled
after an uncle of the present owner
of Antonio's. His like was once
commonplace on both the North
and South Sides of Saint Louis
where recently arrived im-
migrants from Central Europe
congregated.

But not all of this building ornamentation is of such majestic or classical intent. Some is delightfully whimsical.

Bevo Fox, Bevo Building
Broadway and Arsenal Street
Anheuser-Busch Brewing
Company
The fox, always depicted as the
wiliest of animals in medieval
European folk tales, was chosen as
the symbol for Bevo, the non-
alcoholic drink produced by the
Anheuser-Busch Company during
the prohibition era. It is the only
tangible reminder of that period
left in the city.

Saint Louis Water Towers

Although the usefulness of water towers has long since disappeared, these relics of the past continue to be admired for their character and beauty. They serve as favorite landmarks in their areas and any proposals to raze them have - at least so far - been indignantly squelched.

Bissell Water Tower (1889)
Modeled after a Moslem minaret.
Designer: Henry Flad, second in command to Eads during building of Eads Bridge; also one of chief engineers of Saint Louis' water works.

North Grand Water Tower (1871)
Architect: George I. Barnett.
Tallest Corinthian column in the world. Modeled after an ancient Roman Victory Memorial Column.

Romanesque water tower (1894)
Architect: George Mann, one of the architects of the Saint Louis City Hall.
Reservoir Park - looking a bit like a fairy-tale castle - a major embellishment of the Compton Heights Neighborhood.

Clocks

Since the invention of clocks, unique ones have beguiled viewers. Some have even attained definite personalities, i.e., Westminster Parliament Clock, London, often called "Big Ben" although that is actually the name of the clock's chimes; the Glockenspiel in Munich which, every day, has thousands of people (mostly tourists) gawking at it as it strikes eleven and knights dash out pursuing each other around and around until one is finally dehorsed with a lance and a cock crows in defiance; the strange little-man clock at Wells Cathedral, England; and the town clock in Graz, Austria, which had to be ransomed by the townspeople from Napoleon's soldiers bent on destroying it. These, and others of equal unusualness, have fascinated generations.

Saint Louis cannot boast anything of this caliber. Most of its public timepieces are just that—recording the irrevocable passage of the hours. But there are a few exceptions that merit attention . . .

When the downtown area of the city was the only place for serious shopping, Saint Louis' most elegant jewelry store was Mermod, Jaccard and King. Adding to the store's elegance was this imposing clock at its Locust Street entrance. With the move to the outlying shopping centers, the store moved too, finally closing its downtown store.

In the due course of events, the clock, with its air of élan, was moved to Laclede's Landing.

Atomic clock (looking somewhat like the monolithic slabs of granite in the movie classic, "2001, A Space Odyssey") at the east entrance of Boatmen's Bank, is the first commercially displayed atomic time standard in the world. It, and a similar one at the bank's west entrance, are identical to those maintained by the United States and the governments of other nations. The clock is accurate to 1.11 millionth of a second and will maintain that accuracy to within a plus or minus of one second for 4500 years (one cannot help but wonder who will be there to observe it).

Almost all of the outlying suburbs that surround the city of Saint Louis have at least one building from the past that has been preserved and restored by the citizens of the community to help remember its yesterdays.

rail passenger station

Kirkwood Depot

Kirkwood's birth in 1853 was due to the construction of the Missouri Pacific Railroad (originally called the Pacific Railroad). Shortly after the land was surveyed for the new railroad, forty prominent Saint Louis businessmen formed an organization to purchase land near the Des Peres Post Office. Naming the area Kirkwood in honor of James Kirkwood, chief engineer for the Pacific Railroad and responsible for choosing the route the railroad was to follow, the group soon began selling lots.

Train service, citing easy and inexpensive transportation to the city, was heavily featured in the publicity, along with the pleasures of country living. Eventually twenty round trips a day were required to handle the wage earners and lady shoppers going into the city. (The ride to downtown took just thirty-five minutes.)

The present depot, built in 1893, stands on approximately the same site as the original one of the 1850's. Recently restored, it now serves as an Amtrak Station as well as being used for various community happenings. And it is one of Kirkwood's many pleasing-to-the-eye structures.

Rock House

EDGEWOOD CHILDREN'S CENTER
330 North Gore Avenue
Webster Groves

The Rock House, oldest building in Webster Groves, and the present Administration Building for the Edgewood Children's Center, was built in 1850 for the Reverend Artemus Bullard for his newly founded Webster College for Boys (and from which Webster Groves derives its name). Bullard, who came here in 1838 from New England to be pastor of the First Presbyterian Church, was one of the outstanding ministers of his time. Among his numerous accomplishments, he was the first public personage to denounce duelling, then the accepted method of settling even the most trivial of quarrels. He was also an ardent abolitionist.

Because of Bullard's stand on slavery, the isolation of the school and a tunnel in the basement of the Rock House with an exit several blocks away near the railroad tracks, it is now generally believed that one of the functions of the school may have been to serve as a way station in the Underground Railroad that flourished in the county in pre-Civil War times to help runaway slaves make their way to freedom.

Unfortunately, not too much is known about the local Underground Railroad which, although it was an active force, has never been documented. What is known today has only come down by word of mouth.

In the 1890's the exit to the tunnel was sealed off after two children were lost in it and, according to the story passed down about the tragedy, died before being rescued.

Saint Stanislaus Museum
700 Howdershell Road
Florissant.
This building was constructed as a Jesuit Seminary in 1849 by seminarians and brothers to replace a log structure built in 1832 by eight missionaries who had come here from Belgium.

On its 1,200 acres, Saint Stanislaus was a completely self-sufficient entity until 1971 when the seminary was closed due to declining enrollment. Most of the structures were sold at that time except this one original building, which now serves as a museum of Jesuit history.

Especially notable in the collection are the gold, silver and bejeweled monstrances. Some of the other religious art objects on display date back to the fifteenth century.

One of the most famous of all the Jesuits to be trained at Saint Stanislaus was Father Peter DeSmet who was also one of the original missionaries. He was especially well known for his compassionate work among the Indians of the West, who respected and admired him and was known affectionately by them as "Black Robe."

Among his many accomplishments (he was one of the founders of Saint Louis University) was discovering gold in 1840 at Alder Gulch in the Dakotas where the stream ran golden at times. He told no one of this discovery so as not to bring in the gold-seeking hordes that he knew would displace the Indians. It seems odd but is true that the trappers who frequented the region looking for wealth in furs, never paid the slightest attention to the water that gleamed in the sunshine.

Deer skin coat on exhibit at museum was given to DeSmet in 1842 at a Lokota Sioux ceremony. The following are the words of the chief on this occasion: "Black Robe, this is the happiest day of our lives for today for the first time we see among us a man who comes so near to the Great Spirit. Here are the principal braves of our tribe. I have bidden them to a feast we have prepared for you that they may never lose the memory of this so happy day."

(And then they all dined on the tribe's choicest dogs!)

Lake School
Coeur de Ville Drive
Creve Coeur.
Several outlying, one-time rural communities have restored former one-room school houses such as the Lake School in Creve Coeur, which is now a museum of early rural school history.

Although these schools, teaching grades one through eight in a single room and with but one teacher, seem unbelievably primitive today, many of the nation's leaders and brightest citizens of a couple of generations ago attended just such schools.

Payne-Gentry House
4211 Fee Fee Road
Bridgeton.
Typical small town, nineteenth-century, Missouri house (1870), built for Mary Elizabeth and Elbridge Payne, both descendents of early American settlers of North County. For many years it served as the home and office of their grandson, Dr. Will Gentry, a much loved physician of Bridgeton.

Restored by the Bridgeton Historical Society and the City of Bridgeton.

Chinese Pagoda (1873)
Tower Grove Park.
One of the ten gazebos designed by Henry Shaw for his Tower Grove Park. Shaw, on his European travels, was much taken with the fanciful gazebos he saw there. Thus, in his planning of Tower Grove Park, he had these gazebos built that were adaptations of some he had especially admired. He called them "structures for posterity to afford shelter from showers and sunshine (there were then only two trees in all of what was to become Tower Grove Park) and provide places where a drink of refreshing water could be had." They have been delighting parkgoers ever since.

The Ruins
Tower Grove Park.
Another of Shaw's whimsical fantasies, these ruins were patterned after those often found in English gardens of the period to achieve the desired melancholy look.

Shaw's ruins were fashioned from scorched stone blocks found in the debris of the Lindell Hotel fire (1869).

Public Art

Thomas Biddle was killed in a duel on Bloody Island, August 30, 1831, by Spencer Pettis, congressman from this district. Pettis was also killed in the encounter.

Biddle had horsewhipped Pettis for remarks the latter had made in his election campaign about Biddle's brother, Nicholas, president of the Bank of America. After his election Pettis challenged Biddle to a duel, then a commonplace way to settle disputes.

The first statuary to be done by a local artist are these two bas reliefs of Thomas and Anne Mullanphy Biddle, commissioned in the 1840's for the Biddle tomb. Originally at Tenth and Biddle Streets on the grounds of the orphanage established by Mrs. Biddle, the tomb is now located in Calvary Cemetery.
Sculptor: Albert Waugh.

Anne Mullanphy Biddle, widow of Thomas Biddle and daughter of John Mullanphy, Saint Louis' first millionaire, spent the rest of her life and fortune in charitable works. She was the first American woman to be proposed for sainthood in the Roman Catholic Church.

It is sometimes claimed that Saint Louis has more public statuary than any other U.S. city with the exception of New York and Washington. For, from fairly early in the development of the city, Saint Louis had benefactors who wished to either beautify the city or establish a memorial of some kind, by providing funds for various works of sculpture in the city parks or other public areas.

These statues must be viewed in the context of their times in order to be understood and appreciated, for not all of them by any stretch of the imagination can be considered "good art" by today's standards. But they are a part of the history of the city. Each has a story to tell. But as time passes and their stories forgotten, the statues become meaningless. They serve only as part of the scenery with seldom a glance of understanding—or even curiosity—coming their way.

Life-size statue of Daniel Webster given to the Mercantile Library in 1855
Artist: Louis Verhaagen
Donor: H.H. Bacon.
Webster visited Saint Louis in 1837 when at the heighth of his powers and popularity. This visit made a favorable impression on the populace of the city.

One of the more unusual works of art in the Mercantile Library collection is the death mask of Napoleon Bonaparte made shortly after his death, May 5, 1821, at St. Helena, by Dr. Franceso Antonmarchi, his personal physician.

Given to the library in 1847, this copy is one of twelve cast in 1830 by L. Richard et Quesnal under the authorization of Louis Phillipe, King of France (1830-1848). The only other one in the U.S. is at the Cabildo, New Orleans.
Donor: George Hutches Bellasis who was on St. Helena in 1821.

Mercantile Library Association Treasures

Before Saint Louis had an art museum or public parks to beautify, the Mercantile Library Association, founded in 1846 and still one of the oldest subscription libraries in the Mid-west, served as the city's main cultural institution. Many distinguished persons spoke in its auditorium which seated over 2000; its loanable books numbered in the thousands; and an excellent art collection was assembled through the gifts of generous donors.

American bald eagle from James Audubon's four volume, elephant folio THE BIRDS OF AMERICA. The set was purchased by the library for $800.00 in 1858 from Mrs. Nicholas Berthoud, Audubon's sister-in-law, to whom Audubon had given it as a gift.

The affectionate autograph to her was carefully erased by the seller thinking this would enhance the value. (Needless to say, the library has tried by every means possible to restore it.)

Footnote: An elephant folio set of "The Birds of America" recently commanded over a million and a half dollars in a New York auction sale.

Another notable addition in the late 1850's to the Mercantile Library Art Collection is this figure of Beatrice Cenci by Harriet Hosmer.

A fifteenth-century Italian princess, Beatrice Cenci was sentenced to death for her part in a plot to kill her sadistic father. In this piece, resigned, she awaits her fate on the eve of her execution.

Her dramatic story was made popular by Percy Bysshe Shelley's "The Cenci," once a familiar poem to almost all literate English-speaking people.

Although the statue was an anonymous gift to the library, the donor is generally believed to have been Wayman Crow.

Harriet Hosmer's Statues

In her desire to sculpt, Harriet Hosmer wanted to study anatomy. But because of her sex, she was denied admission to all Eastern medical schools (her home was in Massachusetts). Mr. Crow, father of her boarding school roommate, hearing of her plight, invited her to live with him and his family in Saint Louis and attend the McDowell Medical College which agreed to accept her. Even so, to protect her "delicate female sensibilities" she was required to take her classes apart from the male students.

She studied at McDowell and lived with the Crows for a year (1850). Shortly after leaving Saint Louis, she went to Rome for further study. Here she became the darling of the International Set which frequented that Italian city in considerable numbers throughout the nineteenth century. And it was not long before she began to attain international acclaim for her impressive works of sculpture.

Saint Louis is fortunate in having a number of her statues, for Harriet Hosmer is the first woman in the world to attain a distinguished reputation as a sculptress. That her works are a part of the Saint Louis art scene was due to her continued close friendship with the Crows.

Portrait bust of Wayman Crow, Saint Louis philanthropist; founder of the Saint Louis School of Fine Arts, forerunner of Washington University School of Fine Arts; also one of the founders of Washington University.
Artist: Harriet Hosmer
Washington University Art Collection.

The bust, presented at the 1868 Washington University Commencement Ceremony, was a complete surprise to Mr. Crow. Overcome with emotion, he was unable to utter a word.

Inscription on side of bust: "A Tribute of Gratitude. Harriet Hosmer Rome MDCCCLXVI."

82

Thomas Hart Benton
Artist: Harriet Hosmer
Location: Lafayette Park.
The first public memorial in Missouri, this statue of Thomas Hart Benton, famed statesman and U.S. senator from Missouri for thirty years, was dedicated on May 28, 1868. A gala day for Saint Louis! Businesses and schools were closed. Some forty-thousand people converged on Lafayette Park for the ceremonies. Long speeches were presented; a thirty-gun salute honoring Benton's years in the United States Senate heralded the unveiling. The cords for this were pulled by Jessica Benton Frémont, Benton's daughter, another liberated woman for her time. She was the wife of General John Frémont, known in U.S. history as "The Great Pathfinder" for his explorations of the West.·

The Greek mythological Ariadne mourning her desertion by Thesus whom she had helped to escape from the monstrous Minotaur. (Although the Victorians frowned on nudity in art, they accepted it unhesitatingly if a Greek mythological figure was portrayed.)
Artist: Harriet Hosmer.
Washington University Art Collection; inherited from the collection of the Saint Louis School of Fine Arts which Wayman Crow established as a memorial to his son.

83

The unveiling of the Shakespeare statue in Tower Grove Park on the poet's 314th birthday, April 23, 1878, was another gala day for the city. The crowds gathered, the band played, oratory flowed, a holiday air prevailed and lemonade was served to all. Inscription on statute: "He was not of an age but for all time."

The model for the Falstaff bas relief on the pedestal was Ben DeBar (Falstaff was his favorite role), actor and owner of DeBar's Opera House, one of Saint Louis' main theaters for many years.

The mulberry tree in background was imported by Shaw as a tender shoot from Stratford-on-Avon, England, to honor Adelaide Neilson, famous Shakespearian actress, who had played Saint Louis several times and had been entertained at the park by Mr. Shaw.

Henry Shaw's Legacies

Tower Grove Park Art

The outdoor sculpture tradition that Saint Louis has long enjoyed had its beginnings in the latter years of the last century, when Henry Shaw commissioned a number of statues to enhance Tower Grove Park and the Missouri Botanical Garden, both gifts from Mr. Shaw to Saint Louisans.

Shaw, who came to Saint Louis from England via New Orleans in 1819, a relatively poor young man, made his fortune outfitting western-bound migrants for their long trek plus canny real estate investments. In 1839 he retired from active business, saying he had made enough money for any man. After traveling abroad for ten years, he returned to Saint Louis to spend the rest of his life becoming one of the city's most generous benefactors. His gifts to Saint Louis, which have never been surpassed, endure to this day giving enjoyment to thousands every year.

The three larger-than-life bronze statues which adorn Tower Grove Park were among the first large bronze castings in the United States. All are the work of Ferdinand von Miller of Munich, Germany, Shaw's favorite sculptor, who eventually was to execute most of the statuary commissioned by Shaw.

Statue of Alexander von Humboldt, one of the most noted scientists, philosophers, and authors of his time (1769-1859). Among his many accomplishments: he was the first white man to reach the summit of Mt. Chimbarazo, considered a magnificent feat; an explorer of the Amazon River Valley; established the use of isotherms in map making; studied the origins and courses of tropical storms, as well as being a foremost Egyptologist of the period. In spite of his many contributions to science, he is largely forgotten today. His one remembered legacy is the Humboldt Current (which flows along the west coast of South America) that he discovered.

Dedication day of statue: November 24, 1878.

The Christopher Columbus statue, dedicated October 12, 1886, the 394th anniversary of Columbus' landing in the New World, is the first statue of him to be erected in the United States.

The day was a special event for Saint Louis Italian-Americans who were all invited to the ceremonies.

The side plaques depict LaSalle landing at Cahokia, February 12, 1682 (who remembers that anymore?) and the Columbus landing on October 12, 1492.

85

Copies of Antonio Canova's famous lions at tomb of Pope Clement XIII, Rome, Italy. Tower Grove Park, Grand Avenue Entrance.

A great deal of nineteenth century art (before photography was discovered) was copying the work of famous artists. An artist's talent was often judged by how good a copiest he was.

Doing the Canova lions was an especial favorite to copy; and these copies (some good, some bad) are to be found throughout Europe.

It is more than likely that Shaw got the inspiration for these from ones he saw on his 1851 visit to palatial Chatsworth Manor, England, and whose glorious gardens are said to be the source of Shaw's desire to establish his garden.

The bandstand, another of Shaw's architectural fantasies, surrounded by busts of his favorite composers. Band concerts here are a tradition of long standing.

Former entrance gates 1868-1982 (viewed from inside the garden) to the Missouri Botanical Garden with water lilies in foreground. The Garden is famous in horticultural circles for its water lily research and the development of new species.

Missouri Botanical Garden

(SHAW'S GARDEN)

The intent and wish of Mr. Shaw to provide additional pleasures in the lives of Saint Louisans through his garden has continued to be faithfully fulfilled by succeeding administrators in the century following his death in 1889. Thousands throng the Missouri Botanical Garden every year to enjoy the changing seasons, the birds (who throng it too), the many educational programs, flower shows and amusement events that are offered almost without interruption throughout the year. Few bequests have made such an impact on the lives of so many.

In the 1950's a new master plan was proposed for the enlargement of the Garden's scope and further beautification. The program—still in the process of amplification—has resulted in several new buildings, the development of an Herb Garden, a Fragrance Garden for the blind, charming fountains and so many pieces of sculpture by well-known modern artists that Mr. Shaw's garden has become an outdoor sculpture garden too.

Entrance to the Missouri Botanical Garden is now through the Ridgway Center (dedicated 1982). Modeled after the famous Crystal Palace, a revolutionary building at the time, designed by Joseph Paxton for the 1851 Crystal Palace Exposition, London, England, which Mr. Shaw attended.

Mother and Child
Sculptor: Marcel Rau
Donor: David Barron.

Latzer Memorial Fountain greets the incoming visitor.

Shapleigh Memorial Fountain
South Rose Garden
Artist: Eugene Mackay.
With its constantly varying heights of water, the viewer is able to enter into the inner circle of the fountain and be a participant. To enjoy the fountain's gentle spray on a hot summer day is a happy experience.

Mobile
Artist: Alexander Calder.
Formerly part of the outdoor sculpture at the Mansion House Plaza (now Holiday Riverfront Inn). However, the winds from the river which moved it constantly, made it a potential danger and necessitated its removal from that location.

Bust of Linnaeus, founder of modern botany
Sculptor: Ferdinand von Miller.
Decorating the Linnean House, it is the oldest art work in the Garden.

Zerogee
Sculptor: Paul Granland.

Female
Artist: Sir Henry Moore.
Originally at Lambert Saint Louis International Airport, the statue was moved to the Garden when enlargement of the airport required the space it occupied.

Birds in Flight
Sculptor: R. Walker.

One of the most soul-satisfying additions of the Missouri Botanical Garden Master Plan is the Japanese Garden, "Seiwa-En" (garden of pure, clear harmony and peace). Like all other recent additions and improvements to the Garden, it was made possible through the contributions of generous donors, and, in this case, the co-operation of the Saint Louis Japanese community.

(In above picture, note roof of tea house to right of bridge.)
Designer of Japanese Garden: Loichi Kawana.

Lantern designed to catch the falling snow; part of the plan to have the Japanese Garden serenely beautiful in every season.

Lantern from Japanese Exhibit, 1904 Saint Louis World's Fair. (Japanese garden lanterns are seldom lit; instead, the viewer is invited to provide the illumination with his imagination.)

General Nathaniel Lyon
Location: Lyon Park
Sculptor: Charles Steubenraugh.
On May 11, 1861, in one of the first skirmishes of the war, Lyon, then only a captain, led 6000 Union troops to Camp Jackson (now part of Saint Louis University Campus), to force the surrender of the State Militia encamped there under the command of General Daniel Frost. This surprise attack was the result of the Union leaders being convinced that the pro-Southern militia was planning an attack on the U.S. Arsenal in order to capture the large store of ammunition there to turn over to the Confederate Army.

This statue, formerly on the Camp Jackson site (Grand Avenue and West Pine Boulevard) was moved to its present location when Mrs. Harriet Fordyce, daughter of General Frost, gave sufficient funds to enable Saint Louis University to expand its boundaries to include this area. Which, in an ironic twist of fate, is now known as Frost Campus.

Civil War Monuments

The Civil War—or "The War Between The States" as it was commonly called by Saint Louisans of a Southern bent—was a tragic period for Saint Louis. As Missouri was a border state and Saint Louis a border city within a border state, the sympathies of its citizens were sharply divided. Almost all of the old, prominent, monied families were Southern in their customs as well as their loyalties, while many of the newcomers—especially those from the Eastern states and the Germans who had flocked here in such numbers since the 1840's—were solidly pro-Union.

Early in the war years, Union forces took over both the city and the county imposing martial law which lasted until the end of the conflict. Those of Confederate sympathies were often severely treated and their homes frequently requisitioned for Union soldiers. If infractions were considered sufficiently disloyal, all possessions might be confiscated.

This harsh treatment naturally lead to even deeper resentments by a large part of the populace. And wounds were slow to heal after the war was over. Tangible traces of this difficult period in the city's history exist today in the public statues erected by the two factions.

General Ulysses S. Grant
Sculptor: Robert Bringhurst, Saint Louis' first
professional sculptor
Dedicated: 1888
Location: Tucker Boulevard and Market Streets.

Ulysses S. Grant is the only U.S. president to whom Saint Louis can lay claim, although the years he spent here were probably the most miserable of his life.

In 1843 he came to Jefferson Barracks, fresh from West Point; met and fell in love with Julia Dent, a local belle, and sister of a West Point classmate. Over her father's strenuous objections the two were finally married in 1848. Troubled years followed. In 1854, under a cloud because of his drinking, he left the army and returned to Saint Louis from his West Coast station, to his family whom he had not seen in two years.

He first tried his hand at farming some land near Gravois Road which Julia's father had given to her for a wedding present. Failed. He then tried to manage his father-in-law's plantation, "White Haven." Another failure. His next move was to the city to enter the real estate business. Still another failure. Finally, his brothers, out of charity, and at their father's behest, offered him a job in their leather goods store in Galena, Illinois.

But how fortunate these misfortunes were for the Union Cause. Because when the war broke out, his few ties and shaky position enabled him to enlist in the 21st Illinois Volunteers Company where, due to the shortage of commissioned officers, he was made its commander. The stage was now set for his military genius to blossom; his rise to Commander-in-Chief of all Union Forces; and then two terms as President of the United States.

Hundreds pass this statue daily without realizing that it is a memorial to the man whose military strategies were the ultimate factor in preventing the United States from being carved into two nations (it is mind-staggering to think what world history would be if that had come to pass); and helped to bring about the immediate end to legal slavery in this country.

It was just a ten-year journey from abject poverty and hardships to the highest position in the land—the U.S. Presidency!

Frank P. Blair, Jr.
Sculptor: Wellington Gardener
Location: Entrance to Forest Park,
Lindell Boulevard and Kingshighway.
Dedicated: 1885.

The statue of Frank P. Blair, Jr., soldier and statesman, formerly stood in the middle of the intersection of Lindell Boulevard and Kingshighway but, when the road was redesigned, it was moved to its present location. As this site is not easily accessible except to the occasional walker who might stop to investigate or for the very curious motorist who will park, pay a meter fee and then walk a distance to the statue, Blair's mighty contributions to the State of Missouri, the Abolitionists' Crusade, the United States Government, the U.S. Army and the Union Cause have largely been forgotten by the general public.

Inscription on base: THIS MONUMENT IS RAISED TO COMMEMORATE THE IN-DOMITABLE FREE SOLDIER FROM THE WEST: THE HERALD AND STANDARD BEARER OF FREEDOM IN MISSOURI. THE CREATOR OF THE FIRST VOLUNTEER UNION ARMY IN THE SOUTH, THE SAVIOUR OF THE STATE FROM SECESSION, THE PATRIOTIC CITIZEN-SOLDIER WHO FOUGHT FROM THE BEGINNING TO THE END OF THE WAR. THE MAGNANIMOUS STATESMAN, WHO AS SOON AS THE WAR WAS OVER, BREASTED TORRENT OF PROSCRIPTION TO RESTORE TO CITIZENSHIP THE DISFRANCHISED SOUTHERN PEOPLE AND FINALLY, THE INCORRUPTIBLE PUBLIC SERVANT.

Blair's family home in Washington, D.C. is beautiful Blair House, now owned by the U.S. Government and used to house visiting dignitaries.

Confederate Memorial
Sculptor: George Zolnay
Location: Forest Park near hand ball courts
Dedicated: 1914.
Bronze relief representing a Southern family sending off their only remaining adult male to fight on for the principles they hold so dear.

Every year on Memorial Day appropriate ceremonies are held here by the United Daughters of the Confederacy and other sympathizers of the Southern Cause.

The fervor with which many Saint Louisans espoused the Southern Cause is well expressed in these impassioned words inscribed on the back of the shaft of the Confederate Memorial monument.

TO THE MEMORY
OF SOLDIERS AND SAILORS
OF THE SOUTHERN CONFEDERACY
WHO FOUGHT TO UPHOLD
THE RIGHT DECLARED BY JEFFERSON
AND UPHELD BY THE SWORD OF
    WASHINGTON
WITH SUBLIME SELF-SACRIFICE.

THEY
BATTLED TO PRESERVE
THE INDEPENDENCE OF THE STATES
WHICH WAS WON FROM GREAT BRITAIN
AND TO PERPETUATE THE CONSTITUTIONAL
    GOVERNMENT
WHICH WAS ESTABLISHED BY THE FATHERS

ACTIVATED BY THE PUREST PATRIOTISM
THEY PERFORMED DEEDS OF PROWESS
SUCH AS THRILLED THE HEART OF MANKIND
    WITH ADMIRATION.

FIRST IN THE FRONT OF WAR THEY STOOD
AND DISPLAYED A COURAGE SO SUPERB
THAT IT GAVE A NEW AND BRIGHTER
    LUSTER
TO THE ANNALS OF VALOR.

HISTORY
CONTAINS NO CHRONICLE
MORE ILLUSTRIOUS THAN THE STORY OF
    THEIR ACHIEVEMENTS
AND ALTHOUGH WORN OUT BY CEASELESS
    CONFLICT
AND OVERWHELMED BY NUMBERS THEY
    WERE FINALLY FORCED TO YIELD.
"THEIR GLORY ON THE BRIGHTEST PAGES
PENNED BY POETS AND SAGES
SHALL GO SOUNDING DOWN THE AGES."

"WE HAD SACRED PRINCIPLES TO MAINTAIN
AND RIGHTS TO DEFEND FOR WHICH WE
WERE DUTY BOUND TO DO OUR BEST, EVEN
THOUGH WE PERISHED IN THE ENDEAVOR."
                                    ROBERT E. LEE

So far as the author knows, Saint Louis is the only city in the United States to have monuments commemorating the high principles of both the Confederate and Union Sides so close to each other.

95

"Apotheosis of Saint Louis"
(Louis IX for whom Saint Louis is named)
Sculptor: Charles Niehaus.
The plaster original of the statue stood near the main entrance gate to the Fair at Lindell Boulevard and DeBaliviere Avenue. Later, cast in bronze, it was a gift to the city by the Louisiana Exposition Committee from Fair profits.

$\mathcal{T}$reasures

FROM THE SAINT LOUIS WORLD'S FAIR
APRIL 30 - DECEMBER 1, 1904
OFFICIAL TITLE: LOUISIANA PURCHASE EXPOSITION.

The six-months' duration of the 1904 World's Fair was another golden period for Saint Louis. This exposition, whose *raison d'etre* was the one-hundreth anniversary of the Signing of the Louisiana Purchase Treaty, was one of the great fairs of all time. No other fair has ever surpassed it. Few have equalled it.

The story of this Fair with its fifteen elaborate palaces; exhibit buildings from thirty-three foreign countries; forty-four states and territories; dazzling electrical displays (brand new at the time); the landscaping (the ten-million flowers, sixty-thousand shrubs, nine-thousand deciduous and fifteen-hundred evergreen trees, and five-thousand vines, used to decorate the Fair grounds made for some showy effects); and last, but by no means least, the Pike, the lavish, mile-long entertainment center, is a fascinating story. Tales of the Fair's glories and delights have lived on all these many years, enthralling each new generation.

Seldom noticed by visitors to the Saint Louis City Art Museum is the majestic pediment with its larger-than-life statues representing six periods of art: Classical, Oriental, Gothic, Egyptian, Renaissance and Modern.

"Sculpture," carved in Tennessee marble, is one of the gifts to the city from the profits of the Fair.
Sculptor: Daniel Chester French
Location: West side of main entrance steps, Saint Louis City Art Museum. This was also its site during the Fair when it was made of plaster of Paris, as were all the other 1200 Fair statues.

The statue "Painting," by Louis Saint Gaudens, on east side of entrance steps is a similar gift.

Bas relief in limestone of Michelangelo, one of the twenty-two medallions of great artists and architects adorning frieze of museum.

However, relics in the public domain from the Fair are not many. Especially considering its size and scope. For one of the regulations laid down by the fifty-sixth U.S. Congress in granting permission for Saint Louis to hold a World's Fair (besides not being open on Sundays) was that Forest Park, where the Fair was to be held, must be returned to its former condition within a year of the Fair's closing date. Needless to say, the twelve-months following December 1, 1904, saw a lot of wholesale destruction. But the few relics that do remain continue to enrich the lives of many. Most of these are gifts from the profits of the Louisiana Purchase Exposition.

Saint Louis City Art Museum
(Modeled after the Roman Baths of Caracalla)
Architect: Cass Gilbert. The Palace of Fine Arts, one of the few permanent, fireproof buildings of the Fair, was given to the City of Saint Louis to be an art museum, at the Fair's closing.

Today, one of the city's foremost treasures, the museum attracts large numbers of appreciative visitors.

Mural of the Grand Basin of the Fair, Jefferson Memorial Building. Covered up for years, it was recently restored. Artist: Fred Carpenter.

"Signing the Louisiana Purchase Treaty"
Sculptor: Karl Bitter
Dedicated: April 30, 1913.
In the loggia of the Jefferson Memorial Building, the tablet, cast in bronze, represents Monroe, Livingston and Marbois signing the momentous document April 30, 1803.
(A gift from the Fair's profits.)

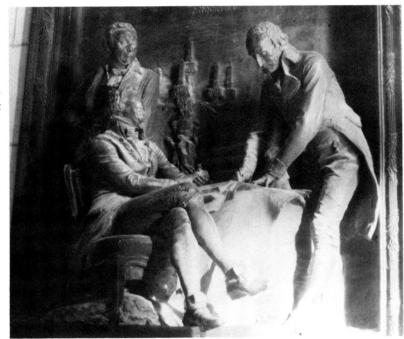

Subject: Thomas Jefferson
Sculptor: Karl Bitter
Dedicated: April 30, 1913.
*Carved from a fourteen-ton marble block **in situ** in the loggia of the Jefferson Memorial Building, the statue, another gift from the Fair's profits, is the first public memorial to Jefferson, third president of the U.S. and responsible for the purchase of the Louisiana Territory from France.*

JEFFERSON MEMORIAL BUILDING

The Jefferson Memorial Building, which stands at the former main entrance gate to the Fair, was also built with profits from the Fair and given to the city in 1913 by the Fair Committee. However, the gift carried with it the understanding that the edifice would forever be the home of the Missouri Historical Society in recognition of the efforts of the society's members in promoting the Fair and helping to insure its success.

WILLIAM K. BIXBY ART GALLERY

Former banquet hall of the British Pavilion fair exhibit; modeled after the famed banquet hall in Kensington Palace, London. The room was incorporated into Bixby Hall (Washington University's School of Fine Arts) when it was completed in 1927.

The British Pavilion, which had served the university as quarters for its art school since the end of the Fair, was destroyed at that time as the "staff" material of which it was constructed was not of a permanent nature.

The room has been used for various purposes over the years including being partitioned into small quarters to provide working studios for student sculptors. Now, returned to its original beauty, it gives the art school a long-needed art gallery of its own.

Footnote: "Staff," a mixture of plaster of Paris, hemp and glue, was the material used for the construction of almost all of the fair's buildings.

The World's Fair Pavilion, still another gift to Saint Louis from the profits of the Fair, was built in 1913 on the former site of the Missouri State Building. The latter, although intended to be a permanent structure, was one of the two buildings destroyed by fire during the Fair's six-months duration. This fire occurred on November 19, too late in the Fair's schedule to be rebuilt.

Friedrich Jahn Memorial, Forest Park
Sculptor: Robert Cauer
Unveiled October 11, 1913
Donors: Saint Louis Chapter of the North American Turnvereins.
Although Jahn, founder of the Turnvereins, never came to North America, his movement had great influence among the many Germans in Saint Louis as well as those elsewhere in the U.S.

This bust is only a part of the Jahn Memorial on the location occupied by the German Pavilion during the Fair.

"Angel of Mercy" stood at the Lindell Skinker Entrance to Fair
Sculptor: Roman Romanelli.
Given to the city by David O'Neil, one of the founders of Forest Park, the statue stood for many years near the lower level entrance to the Municipal Opera where it was badly vandalized. Restored, it is now by Tower Grove House, Shaw's Garden.
(Henry Shaw's country home, Missouri Botanical Garden.)

Mural, University City Post Office. Painted in 1938 as part of a WPA project, it depicts a happy day at the Fair. David R. Francis, its energetic and exuberant president, and Mrs. Francis are the strolling couple. The Ferris wheel in the background, the largest ever to be built, was destroyed by dynamite at the close of the Fair. Domed building on left is "Jerusalem", one of the most popular exhibits at the Fair.

Entrance to Francis Field, Washington University, named to honor David R. Francis.
The 1904 Olympic Games took place here.

Subject: General Friederich von Steuben
Sculptor: Unknown
Location: Tower Grove Park.
German military genius and inspector-general under General George Washington, von Steuben's aid was of immeasurable help to the American Cause during the Revolutionary War.

Statue given by the German Government during the Saint Louis World's Fair. Recently restored and presented to Tower Grove Park by the Richard Barthold Unit No. 28 of the von Steuben Society.

Subject: Young Italian family with all their worldly possessions arriving in the United States to seek a better life.
Sculptor: Rudy Torini
Location: Saint Ambrose Church on "The Hill."
Statue commemorates the many poor Italian immigrants who came to Saint Louis and settled on "The Hill," because it was near the fire clay mines where a majority of the men worked.

"The Hill," English translation for Piedmont (little mountain), the section of Italy from whence most of those living in this area came, is the only true ethnic community surviving in Saint Louis.

The money to commission this statue was raised from the proceeds of the popular "Hill Day," celebrated annually with Italian food, music and games.

In the various museums, parks, libraries, open spaces, on walls, both public and private buildings—all scattered around the city and its environs—are many other works of art. Statues, paintings, rare books, murals and artistic fountains. And all for the public's pleasure and edification. The following are but a few that, for one reason or another, have a special appeal for the author.

Subject: George Washington
Sculptor: Jean Houdon
Location: Lafayette Park.
One of the six bronze castings of the marble, life-size statue of General Washington that stands in the rotunda of the state capitol building in Richmond, Virginia.

The facial portrait is considered one of the best of Washington, as it was done from a plaster cast made by Houdon when he visited Mount Vernon for this purpose.

Beautifully crafted and artistically engraved cannon, cast in Mexico in 1783 for King Charles III of Spain and sovereign of all the Louisianas, is the only tangible relic in Saint Louis of its once being a possession of Spain 1764-1804.
Location: Forest Park.

"The Naked Truth"
Sculptor: William Wandschneider.
Location: Reservoir Park.
Commissioned by a group of German-Americans to honor the three influential editors of the once-famous German newspaper, **The Westlich Post**: Carl Danzer, Emil Preetorious and Carl Schurz.

On the dedication day, May 14, 1914, every German-American Association in the city was represented, with the German flag proudly displayed alongside of the American flag—the last time in the city's history because of the bitterness that soon came with World War I.

The statue was highly controversial for many years because of its nudity.

"Vision"
Sculptor: Walker Hancock
Location: Soldiers' Memorial.
One of four equestrian figures decorating the Soldiers' Memorial, it was the cause of an acrimonious dispute during its carving. The child held by the female figure was not in the original contract but so strongly did the stone carver, Alex Baretta, feel that it was necessary to the spirit of the design, that he assumed the extra $1000 cost himself.

A former Saint Louisan, Sculptor Walker Hancock was assigned during World War II to protect art in the European Zone. He saved the hidden treasures of Charlemagne, a vast collection of German medieval art, and found the bodies of Frederick the Great and his father, Frederic William I, in a German salt mine.

Subject: Pierre de Laclede de Liguest (circa 1724-1778), founder of Saint Louis
Sculptor: George Zolnay
Donor: Saint Louis Centennial Association
Location: Washington Park (between Saint Louis Municipal Courts Building and City Hall).
Unveiled May 30, 1914, the statue depicts Laclede as he steps ashore from his pirogue onto a wilderness river bank (later the foot of Market Street) on a cold December day in 1763, and chose this favorable site for his future settlement.

One of five bronze castings of statue discovered in the eighteenth century in the ruins of Herculaneum, Roman city destroyed by volcanic lava from Mount Vesuvius in 79 A.D.

Original in National Museum, Naples, Italy.
Location: Cupples House Garden.
Donor: Mrs. Caroline Humbolt Burford.

"Moby Dick"
Sculptor: Dimitri Stoyanoff.
Swimming pool on the grounds of former home of E.G. Lewis, founder of University City. In the background is an old-time garden ornament which marks the spring head from whence early University City residents obtained their drinking water. The spring still exists but is channeled into University City's sewer system.

Easter Island Heads
Location: Museum of Science and Natural History.
Although only replicas of the enormous heads on Easter Island, these are fascinating to contemplate because of the tantalizing mysteries surrounding the origin and purpose of the originals.

Subject: Pope Pius XII. Note right hand of statue is raised in the ancient, traditional symbol of the Praetor (teacher in authority)
Sculptor: Ivan Mestrovic
Location: North entrance of Pius XII Memorial Library, Saint Louis University.
The library is famed for its extensive microfilm collection of rare manuscripts and books from the Vatican Library, the only collection of this material outside of Rome.

Robert Burns
Sculptor: Robert Aitken
Location: Washington University Campus
Donor: Robert Burns Society. (Club still sponsors an annual Scottish Celebration Evening on Burns' birthday.)

One of the hand-colored illustrations by William Blake, visionary poet and artist, for the famous 1795 edition of Edward Young's **Night Thoughts On Immortality**. *From the William K. Bixby rare books collection, Washington University's Special Collections Library.*

Bear inspired by the Missouri State Seal
Sculptor: Victor S. Holm. Holm served as professor of sculpture for twenty-six years (1909-1935) at the Washington University School of Fine Arts
Location: Kiel Auditorium.

Saint Francis of Assisi
Sculptor: Carl Mose
Location: Jewel Box, Forest Park.

When first unveiled, a controversy arose over having the statue of a Roman Catholic saint in a public park. But the final consensus of Saint Louisans was that Saint Francis, a universal saint and the world's first known animal conservationist, was worthy of a place of honor in the hearts of all.

Fountain inspired by old Italian well-heads
Sculptor: Nancy Koonsman Hahn
Donor: Margaret Kinkaid of Louisiana, Missouri
Location: Lucas Park.
The land for this park on Locust Street between Thirteenth and Fourteenth Streets was given to the city in 1857 by James Lucas in memory of his father, Judge John J.B. Lucas. (The latter, an early prominent citizen of Saint Louis, was sent here in 1805 by President Jefferson to serve as land commissioner to settle Spanish Land Grant claims.)

In the first years of this century the city authorities planned to install a watering trough for horses here. On further consideration, however, a decision was reached that it would be more in keeping with Mr. Lucas' wishes if the park was used for the relaxation of people instead of horses. This charming fountain is the substitute for the watering trough.

Fountains

Another serendipitous aftermath of the Louisiana Purchase Exposition was the public fountains beautifying the cityscape that were now possible. For the excellent water that Saint Louis has long enjoyed was a direct result of a plan forced upon the city officials to authorize a series of filtering basins for the water systems, so that the water falls—planned to be in front of Festival Hall and the two attendant buildings (one of the Fair's outstanding features and a stunning visual experience for all fairgoers) might have crystal clear water. Up until that time the city water came directly from the Mississippi River, mud and all. It is a reasonable assumption that at sometime during the past eighty-odd years Saint Louis would have improved its water system. But the Fair forced the issue in 1904.

Fountain in Forest Park on the former location of the Fair's U.S. Government Building.
During the day hours, this is just an ordinary fountain cascading water into the air. At night, with many different colored lights blending one into another, playing upon the varying heights of water, it becomes a magical one.

The lake in the background, drained for the Fair to be a sunken garden, was popular as a meeting place and for resting weary feet. It separated the Liberal Arts Palace and the Palace of Mines and Metallurgy.

Subject: "The Runner"
Sculptor: William Zorach
Location: Kiener Plaza.

Henry Kiener, a member of the 1904 Olympics track team, left a substantial sum of money in his will for a work of sculpture to be placed in a public area that was to depict the sport of running.

At first the bequest posed a problem for it was a period when abstract art was at its peak of importance. Few artists of stature were willing (or able) to do representational art. The difficulty was solved when William Zorach, although well known for his abstract sculpture, was engaged to do a fountain piece that would conform to the strictures of the Kiener will.

Now a general favorite and photogenic too, "The Runner" provides the background for hundreds of photographs taken annually by visitors to Saint Louis.

Subject: "Creation"
Sculptor: Andre Demtrovic
Location: Northwest Plaza, one of the first shopping centers in the nation to be developed around the principle that beauty is commercially profitable.

Fountain near Jewel Box, Forest Park
Donor: The Missouri Society of Colonial Daughters.
A number of the fountains around the city do nothing more than add a pleasant, soothing note to the environment. For flowing water, a symbol of life since the most ancient of times, seems to fulfil a deep need of mankind.

Inscription on base of "The Dying Leaf" Fountain.

"Dying Leaf" Fountain
Sculptors: Saunders Schultz, William Severson
Location: Bee Tree Park.
Featuring a fallen ginkgo leaf, this fountain is dedicated to Saint Louis businessman, Lindell Gordon, who, though terminally ill, instigated and helped bring about the purchase of this large tract of land overlooking the Mississippi River for a park to be enjoyed by all.

Now, with its spectacular view of the river, the thousands of daffodils that bloom on the hillsides in the spring, the picnic areas, the woodland trails and the Golden Eagle River Museum, Bee Tree Park is one of the most frequented of the county parks.

Maryland Plaza Fountain, Central West End.
Saint Louis' long-time mayor, Alfonzo Cervantes (1965-1973), loved the fountains of Rome and tried to have more built in his own city. This, typical of the kind found in many old world cities, is one.

"Falling Man" Fountain
Sculptor: Ernest Trova
Location: Plaza of Holiday Riverfront Inn (formerly Mansion House).
When the Mansion House was built, financed by government funds, regulations required that a certain percentage of the money must be spent on art works. The plaza—by whatever name—has been, since its completion, one of the city's finest art walks.

"The Meeting of the Waters"   *Sculptor: Carl Milles*   *Location: Aloe Plaza.*

This bronze fountain group by Carl Milles was originally to be named "The Wedding of the Rivers" to symbolize the confluence of the Mississippi and the Missouri Rivers a short distance north of Saint Louis. But when the plaster casts were first unveiled, an uproar arose over the virile nudity of the bridegroom and the demure coyness of the bride. In deference to these modest citizens, the name was changed to the present one at the time of the final unveiling (1941).

Even then the grumblings continued. Now it was the naiads and Triton, the wedding guests, who drew fire. "What connection is there between Saint Louis and Greek mythological figures?" was the complaint. With the passage of time, however, the fountain, with its blithe, jocund spirit, has become one of the city's best-loved landmarks. For it has what the Greeks called **aglama**, "to fill the soul of the beholder with delight." And to view the fountain on a summer night under a full moon is an experience never to be forgotten.

With the Union Station having little or no traffic for a few years, "The Meeting of the Waters" languished for lack of attention. Few stopped in their passage-by in an automobile to admire it; and there was little reason for people on foot to be in that neighborhood. With the transformation of the deserted station into a bustling shopping center and an elegant hotel, the fountain once again has an appreciative audience.

111

"Wally"
Eighth and Pine Streets.

Outdoor Wall Murals

In the 1970's and '80's in U.S. cities across the land it was realized by officials, private companies and individuals that a way to brighten up drab sections of an area was by colorful wall murals.

Saint Louis, being essentially a brick city with acres of blank, somber walls in its older sections, is especially adaptable to this art form. Now, there are some fifty-odd murals decorating walls all over town. Some are enormous in size. Some are on the small side. Some have social messages. Some are humorous. Some have historical connotations. Some are just decorative. But all are of a cheerful nature portraying a happy scene.

"Grand Arcade"
Delmar Boulevard, University City Loop.
Commissioned by the University City Municipal Arts Commission.

"Soulard"
Lafayette Avenue and Broadway.

"Car Heaven"
Locust Street at Leffingwell Avenue.
Nostalgic mural glorifying the early days of automobiles is a reminder that this section of Locust Street was formerly called "Automobile Row," because so many different makes of automobiles could be purchased here.

"Discovering Hyde Park," Twentieth and Salisbury Streets.

All murals on pages 112, 113, 114 are by "On The Wall Productions, Inc."

"Que sera? Seurat?" or "A Sunday Afternoon in the Park," inspired by the beloved Seurat painting of that name.

Grand Avenue at Arsenal Street.

Part of the "Return to DeBaliviere Avenue's Glory Days" mural. Depicted is the entrance to the Winter Garden, the ice skating rink where several generations of young Saint Louisans learned this skill. The building was originally erected to house the Jai Alai courts during the World's Fair. It was demolished in the rejuvenation of this area due to its bad condition.

Location: 500 DeBaliviere Avenue.

"Aphrodite Rising From The Sea."
Made from bottle caps and broken glass.

Location of murals: Burkhart's
Oyster Bar, 736 South Broadway.
Artist: David Classe.

"Puff, The Magic Dragon."

Pegasus.

"The Wall"
Sculptor: Richard Serra
Site: Civil Courts Plaza.

By far the most controversial of all the local contemporary art is this rusty (on purpose) steel wall. A prime attraction for graffiti, it offers the possibility (according to the artist) of a quiet, sheltered spot away from the turmoil of urban life for either contemplation or a picnic lunch. Said to be at its best when viewed from the upper floors of the Civil Courts Building.

Contemporary Public Art

Representative works of a number of the era's most prominent, acclaimed sculptors have been added to the Saint Louis public art collection in the past quarter century.

However, a question looms large in the minds of many viewers. Is this REALLY art? Or just a gigantic leg pull—excellent examples of more "new clothes for the Emperor?" Only the years ahead will give the final answer.

Works of other equally well-known contemporary sculptors are found in other sections of *"Saint Louis Treasures."*

"The Electric Wall Plug" Sculptor: Claes Oldenburg.   Location: Saint Louis City Art Museum. This is another sculpture that caused outraged cries from the public, especially when it was first placed near the main entrance to the City Art Museum. Now, in the rear of the building amidst luxuriant greenery, it has even become something of a wry favorite even with those who formerly decried it.

"Archean"
Sculptor: Dame Barbara Hepworth
Location: Washington University Campus.

"La Joie de Vivre"
Sculptor: Jacques Lipchitz
Location: Steinberg Skating Rink.

"Les Danseuses"
Sculptors: Saunders Schultz, William C. Severson
Location: Clayton Mercantile Centre, Meramec and Maryland Avenues.

A number of the new office buildings, erected in the rejuvenating building boom that Saint Louis enjoys, have also included stunning sculptures—pleasing to both the eye and spirit of the passerby—as part of their aesthetic architectural designs.

"Competition"   *Sculptor: J. Seward Johnson*   *Location: Saint Louis Centre.*

Life-like statue of Julie Wier of Fairmont, Illinois, chosen as the subject in a contest to discover someone who represented the "Spirit of Saint Louis." Her poem detailing her triumph over Hodgkin's disease, which won her the competition, is inscribed in the notebook on her lap.

"Goxarch #10"
Sculptor: Ernest Trova.
Trova, famous local sculptor, began the collection of contemporary sculpture for Laumeier Park with the donation (and loan) of a number of his pieces.

Laumeier Sculpture Park

On a scenic seventy-five acres overlooking the Meramec Valley, willed to Saint Louis County by Mrs. Henry R. Laumeier to be developed as a passive park, an internationally recognized sculpture garden has been developed that has won gradual and affectionate acceptance by Saint Louisans. Well-attended concerts, Shakespearian plays, ballet productions and other performing arts events take place here on a regular basis throughout the spring, summer and fall. The park is also popular for weddings, kite-flying and just wandering about. The collection of works by contemporary sculptors, all placed throughout the park for maximum environmental impact, is impressive. The wanderer will occasionally come upon a work in the most unlikely spot, which is a part of the pleasure of Laumeier Park. Surprises.

The gabled, Tudor-style mansion, formerly the Laumeier residence, is now an art gallery, which, although featuring modern art, still manages to maintain a warm intimacy.

(An additional twenty-five acres of woodlands was later purchased to add to the original Laumeier bequest.)

"The Grand Striptease"
Sculptor: Giacomo Manzu.

"Untitled"
Sculptor: David Von Schlegell.

Easily the best-loved by the citizenry of all the local contemporary sculpture is the soaring, stainless steel Gateway Arch which looms massively but with matchless grace on the Mississippi River front. The result of a nation-wide competition won by Architect Eero Saarenin, the ground-breaking for the Arch was in April, 1961; the keystone was put in place on October 29, 1965, accompanied by a jubilant, citywide celebration.

As a symbol of Saint Louis when it was the "Gateway to the West" for the many thousands of migrants who passed through on their way to seek new opportunities or adventures, the Arch is the focal point of the Jefferson National Expansion Memorial which occupies the downtown river front. In the base of the Arch is an extra-ordinary museum which graphically depicts the struggles and triumphs of this great movement that peopled the West. Now one of the most visited tourist attractions of the world, the Arch is also synonymous world-wide with the City of Saint Louis.

"Architecture should, among other things, fulfil man's belief in the nobility of his existence."
Eero Saarenin

Footnote: Photo taken from Holiday Inn Riverfront Plaza; sculpture in foreground is by Lawrence Marcell.

Memorial Art
in
Bellefontaine Cemetery
and
Calvary Cemetery

Heartbreak in Stone (Calvary Cemetery)

Memorial art reached its zenith during the latter years of the nineteenth century and the early ones of the twentieth and was a definite part of the excessive mourning customs of this time: The long periods of bereavement inflicted on families which permitted few outside activities and no entertainment; the somber, black widow weeds, often worn for the remainder of the widow's lifetime; the gloomy paintings and needlework depicting death; the hair wreaths made from the hair of the departed holding a place of honor in the parlor. These, along with countless other now archaic rites, were all well-observed mourning conventions of the period. Even horticulture was affected by this preoccupation with death, as weeping willows became a favorite of the gardening world because their drooping leaves seemed to be an expression of profound sorrow.

The many elaborate, fanciful and often poignant memorials at both Bellefontaine and Calvary Cemeteries are, of course, but other expressions of this important fashion. These memorials served as status symbols too, to be admired by the many visitors who came on a fairly regular basis to the cemeteries during this era.

Carved marble angel head decorating the Yeatman Memorial.

122

Memorial (Bellefontaine Cemetery) to Henry Shreve (1787-1851), "Master of the Mississippi." After Shreve finally broke the Livingston-Fulton river monopoly (circa 1819) that had stifled the growth of steamboat transportation for many years, he set about building the first practical boat for use on the Mississippi River.

Later, under contract from the War Department, Shreve, with a boat he invented for the purpose, cleared the Mississippi River of the logs and driftwood that were a hazard to its river traffic. But Shreve's special claim to fame in the annals of American history is for opening up the Red River for navigation (claimed to be impossible by all experts). So dense were the rafts of driftwood, logs and other debris that had collected in many places on the Red River that people, with loaded wagons and horses, were able to cross safely over, totally unaware of the flowing water beneath them.

A number of Celtic crosses, much admired by those of Scottish or Irish ancestry, are found in both cemeteries. This cross in Bellefontaine Cemetery memorializing James MacCash, founder of the Scottish clans in Saint Louis in 1871, is one of the most imposing.

It must be remembered that during the Victorian Age cemeteries served a far different purpose than today. For in that period of large families, heavy mortality rates and far fewer recreational activities, Sunday afternoon visits to the family grave plots were routine in many households. And, as there were few parks, others also came to stroll about enjoying the trees and foliage, and to admire the imposing memorials. Strange as it may now seem to the present generation, going to the cemetery for a pleasant afternoon was a commonplace leisure time activity.

Bellefontaine and Calvary Cemeteries, two of the city's oldest and most venerable cemeteries, were designed with these customs in mind. And in them are to be found some of Saint Louis' greatest treasures, both artistically and historically.

Gothic style tombstone of John Mullanphy (1758-1833) and his son Bryan (1808-1851), Calvary Cemetery.
Irish-born John fought with the Irish Brigade for Louis XVI during the French Revolution. After the Royalists lost, he and his family migrated to the United States, finally arriving in Saint Louis in 1808.
Saint Louis' first millionaire, John made his fortune by cornering the cotton market at the end of the War of 1812, a large part of which he subsequently invested in Saint Louis real estate. Eccentric but philanthropic, he left a profound impression on Saint Louis.
Bryan, equally eccentric, serving as mayor of Saint Louis during the 1849 cholera epidemic, was so moved by the suffering of the migrants caught here during this terrible time that he left a substantial part of his fortune to assist travelers in distress. This helped to bring about the eventual founding of the Travelers' Aid Society.

Carved buffalo head, one of the several stone likenesses of animals that once inhabited the Far West which decorate the Clark Memorial. It is also a memorial to the buffalo whose enormous herds, often numbering in the millions, roamed the prairies when Lewis and Clark led their expedition westward. Less than a hundred years later the species faced extinction; only strong conservation efforts saved it.

WILLIAM CLARK
BORN IN VIRGINIA
AUGUST 1, 1770
ENTERED INTO LIFE ETERNAL
SEPTEMBER 1, 1838
SOLDIER, EXPLORER,
STATESMAN AND PATRIOT
HIS LIFE IS WRITTEN
IN THE HISTORY OF HIS COUNTRY.

Subject: General William Clark
Sculptor: William Partridge
Location: Bellefontaine Cemetery.

Clark was co-leader with Meriwether Lewis of the Lewis and Clark Expedition which opened up the West for the United States and which is generally considered one of the great explorations of history. The expedition left Saint Louis May 17, 1804, and returned September 19, 1806. As the expedition had not been heard from for such a long time, the men on it had been given up as dead. Their eventual return was the cause of much rejoicing and celebrating.

Clark also served as Territorial Governor of Missouri (1813-1821) and later was Superintendent of Indian Affairs with headquarters in Saint Louis (1821-1838). The affection, trust and respect the Indians had for Clark (to whom he was known as "Red Head") was responsible for many of the early peaceful settlements between the Indians and the U.S. Government.

His youngest son, Jefferson Clark, left money in his will for this imposing monument to his father. Its unveiling and dedication was one of the important ceremonies that took place during the summer of the World's Fair.

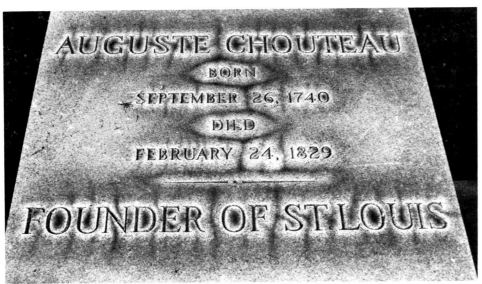

In the early 1920's some of Auguste Chouteau's descendents ordered a new tombstone to be made for his grave, as the original has disintegrated with age. Desirous of having their ancestor be of a more likely age to be co-founder of Saint Louis (he was only thirteen when he accompanied Laclede up the river in 1763) they authorized having his birthdate moved back ten years on the new tombstone. One problem with this ploy, however, was that it made his mother but seven-years old at the time of his birth! (Calvary Cemetery)

Both Bellefontaine and Calvary Cemeteries were established in the middle of the last century. Bellefontaine Cemetery—in 1849 by a group of prominent Saint Louis business men of various Protestant faiths; Calvary Cemetery, in 1857, directly alongside of it, by the Roman Catholic Archdiocese of Saint Louis.

As the city had just suffered a devastating cholera epidemic which had taxed all existing facilities, the planners of both cemeteries purchased sufficient ground to take care of the city's needs for several centuries in case of a similar catastrophe. In the due course of time, as the City of Saint Louis needed additional land for its growth, all cemeteries within the city limits were moved to either one cemetery or the other depending on the religious beliefs of the deceased. As a consequence, the history of Saint Louis from its beginning to the present, as well as that of much of the Western Expansion Movement, is recorded here on the tombstones of the men and women who helped to write it.

Manuel Lisa (1772-1820), one of the most colorful of the early fur traders, and influential in the opening up of the West for exploration.

His Saint Louis wife, Mary Hempstead Lisa, one of the seven original founders of the First Presbyterian Church of Saint Louis (and Mother Church of all other local Presbyterian churches) was the first white woman to venture up the Missouri River into Indian Territory. His Osage Indian wife, Mitain, came to Saint Louis after Lisa's death and the two women lived amicably together bringing up Lisa's two half-Indian children.

The Lisa grave is now in the oldest part of Bellefontaine Cemetery, originally his wife's family burial grounds on the Hempstead farm. Also in this plot are Mary's father, Stephen Hempstead, who fought under Nathan Hale in the American Revolution; and her brother Edward, Missouri's first Territorial Representative in Congress. The latter is credited as being one of the founders of the Saint Louis public school system for his introduction of a bill in Congress allotting to the Saint Louis schools all untitled land within the city limits of 1812.

General Stephen Watts Kearny, prominent military leader of the nineteenth century. He fought with distinction in the War of 1812; was a long-time commander at Fort Leavenworth protecting the wagon trains enroute to Oregon; and a pacifier of the Indians. But he is best remembered for his exploits during the Mexican War. After leading his men safely through the "Great American Desert," he captured Sante Fe and the Mexican State of New Mexico and set up a civil government to rule the inhabitants. Going on to California, he captured San Diego and Los Angeles from Mexican forces; and then served as military governor of California in the early days of U.S. ownership. Later, he was military governor of Vera Cruz and Mexico City. (Bellefontaine Cemetery).

Dr. William Beaumont, one of the founders of modern medicine through his famed book, **Experiments and Observations on The Gastric Juices and the Physiology of Digestion.** The publication of this book—the result of his treating a young half-breed, Alexis St. Martin, whose shotgun wound in the stomach refused to heal, enabling Beaumont to observe the process of digestion through an opening in St. Martin's abdominal wall—revolutionized knowledge on the subject.

A group of local doctors and the Beaumont High School Choir hold an annual service at his graveside to honor him for his contributions to the field of medicine. (Bellefontaine Cemetery).

Sarcophagus of James Eads, designer of Eads Bridge, one of the engineering marvels of the nineteenth century. The first bridge to span the Mississippi River at Saint Louis and linking the Eastern and Western railroads, it was a true gateway to the West.

Eads was also the designer of the iron-clad boats used by the Union Army during the Civil War and which were instrumental in Grant's successful siege of Vicksburg, a major factor in the Union victory.

Another of Eads' engineering feats was the saving of New Orleans by a design for a series of river piers that shifted the Mississippi River back to the New Orleans harbor (said to be impossible by the Army Corps of Engineers) which was being left high and dry by the changing river channel.

Bellefontaine Cemetery

With winding roads, grassy knolls, a lake and a wide variety of trees—many non-native—Bellefontaine was designed as a romantic landscaped park by its first superintendent, Almerin Hotchkiss, who came here in 1850 from a famous Eastern cemetery noted for its natural beauties. The collection of trees he assembled—with the assistance of Henry Shaw—is considered one of the finest in America. In the spring time the cemetery is a mass of fairy-like bloom; in autumn the brilliant coloring is breath-taking.

And the roster of Bellefontaine Cemetery reads like a "Who's Who" of Americana: William H. Danforth, founder of the Ralston Purina Company; John Queeny, founder of Monsanto Chemical Company; his son Edgar who made the company of world-wide importance; James McDonnell, founder of McDonnell Aircraft Company; William S. Burroughs, founder of the Burroughs Adding Machine Company; James Eads, designer and engineer of Eads Bridge; Adolphus Busch, founder of Anheuser-Busch Brewery Company; Frank Rand and Jackson Johnson, founders of International Shoe Company; George Brown, founder of Brown Shoe Company; Robert Brookings, partner of Samuel Cupples, president of Washington University and founder of the renowned Brookings Institute; John Gregg, inventor of the Gregg Shorthand System which revolutionized business the world over.

The above are just a fraction of the names that are important in the business world. Then there are those who helped to write the history of this nation in other fields. Explorers, statesmen, mountain men, soldiers, authors, artists, river men. Even a few liberated women far ahead of their times. The list goes on and on to include many other men and women who also made invaluable contributions to the development of the United States (and Saint Louis).

General Richard Mason, early military and civil governor of California. His sarcophagus was designed by John Struther, another renowned nineteenth-century designer of memorial art. Struther's best-known work is the George and Martha Washington tomb at Mount Vernon, now a national shrine.

Mason died of yellow fever at Jefferson Barracks in 1850. In the same plot is the grave of General Don Carlos Buell, Union Army general, and second husband of Mason's widow.

Hamilton Gamble (1798-1864) appointed Provisional Governor of Missouri to serve during the Civil War years, after the flight of Governor Claiborne Jackson to the Confederacy. The two shafts joined together by the wreath of peace is symbolic of his holding together the two conflicting sides during that troubled period.

General Sterling Price (1809-1867), one-time governor of Missouri (1853-57), fought for the Confederate Side throughout the war. Troops under his command won several battles in Missouri but his defeat at the Battle of Westport (1864) virtually ended the Civil War in Missouri. He fled then to Mexico to serve in the Army of Emperor Maximillian. After the latter's execution, Price, at the behest of his many friends in Saint Louis, returned here.

His funeral was one of the largest ever held in the city.

One of the most unusual of all the monuments in Bellefontaine Cemetery is this piece of the Plymouth Rock brought here by the Edward Chases, when the family migrated to Saint Louis from the East in the 1830's.

Taken from the original rock before it held such a sacred place in American history, it was not considered a desecration to usurp this portion of one of the nation's greatest historical treasures. In fact the Chases were especially proud of it.

Child's grave from 1850's in Charless-Blow lot. Nearby is the grave of Taylor Blow, owner of Dred Scott and who gave Scott his freedom after the latter's case was lost in the U.S. Supreme Court.

A copy of Napoleon's tomb at the Invalides, Paris.

Samuel Hawken, gunsmith. The Hawken Rifle, manufactured by him and his brother Jacob, was the favorite of mountain men and explorers and another significant factor in the opening of the West.

Portrait of Samuel Bagnell, one of the three Bagnell surveyor brothers for whom Bagnell Dam was named.

On the Yeatman obelisk is this portrait of Angelica Yeatman who died in the 1849 cholera epidemic. The sculptor, Robert Von der Launitz, was considered the foremost memorial artist of the time.

Husband James (1810-1901), outstanding civic-minded nineteenth-century Saint Louisan, was one of the founders of the Western Sanitary Commission (1861). This organization was the first of its kind in the world to be dedicated to the tending of wounded, sick and dying soldiers in hospitals and war prisons (it predated the Red Cross by several years).

Minor Family Tombstone

Virginia Minor, wife, (1823-1895) lawyer and feminist, brought suit against the Saint Louis Election Commissioners for refusing her voting privileges (1872). With her husband's help (also a lawyer), she fought the case all the way to the U.S. Supreme Court where the nine judges unanimously decided that regardless of what the Fourteenth Amendment stated, it did not include voting rights for women. However, although she lost her case, the publicity was helpful to the suffragette cause.

Sara Teasdale, one of the nation's best-known female poets, writing mainly about unrequited love, won the first Pulitzer Prize ever awarded for poetry (1918).

Found drowned in her bathtub, it was never known whether the death was accidental or a suicide.

Monument to those from unmarked graves moved here from an old Protestant Cemetery between Franklin (now Martin Luther King Drive) and Washington Avenues. The sarcophagus is copied from the horned altars of ancient Biblical times; fugitives seeking sanctuary there were secure, even from the wrath of kings, as long as they grasped the horns of the altar.

Many imposing and handsome obelisks adorn Bellefontaine Cemetery. This one marks the plot of a branch of the Griesediecks, an important brewery family.

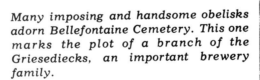

Marble shaft to the memory of the Reverend Alexander Van Court, first pastor of Central Presbyterian Church.
Building on shaft is a replica of the first building of the congregation which stood on northwest corner of Locust and Eighth Streets. It was ready for dedication when Van Court died in July, 1849, another victim of the cholera epidemic.

"Death"
Sculptor: George Zolnay.
Memorial of David R. Francis (1850-1927), energetic president of the Louisiana Purchase Exposition, whose charismatic leadership and vision were responsible for much of the success of this most successful of World Fairs.

Francis also served as mayor of Saint Louis (1885-1889); governor of Missouri (1889-1893); Cleveland's Cabinet (1896-1897). He was Ambassador to Russia during the October 1917 Revolution; his memoirs of these momentous days are important eyewitness accounts of that historical event.

Close-up of the serene but sad face of "Death."

Detail from Bridge tomb.

Tomb of Hudson E. Bridge, wealthy manufacturer and philanthropist.

133

Christ Von Der Ahe, owner of the first Saint Louis Browns Baseball Team, had his larger-than-life-size statue with the date of his birth - 1851 - and the date of his death - 1913 - erected several years before his demise. As he foretold, he died in 1913.

In Bellefontaine Cemetery, as in all cemeteries, there is a wonderful collection of human interest stories.

Kate Brewington Bennett, a beauty of her time, was especially noted for her alabaster-white skin. After her unexpectedly sudden death, it was discovered she took a daily dose of arsenic to maintain her admired pallor, not knowing that its effects were cumulative.

In the early years of this century Herman Luyties, drug manufacturer, went to Italy on a combination business and pleasure trip. There, so the story goes, he fell in love with a voluptuous Italian model. Unable to bring her home, he had her likeness carved in Carrara marble and shipped back to Saint Louis where he ensconced it in the foyer of his home at 33 Portland Place. (His wife left him ere long.)

In time - because the weight of the marble was causing structural problems - Luyties had the statue moved to Bellefontaine Cemetery to a plot purchased especially for it. And eventually him. Buried at her feet in 1921, Bessie (as she is called by the cemetery attendants) maintains an eternal vigil over his grave.

Captain Isaiah Sellers (1802-1864), one of the best-known riverboat men of his era. His knowledge of the Mississippi River was prodigious; it was claimed that he could be called up to the pilot house from his stateroom at any time of the day or night and know the exact location of the boat.

He wrote shipping notes under the **nom de plume** of Mark Twain; upon his death the name was adopted by Samuel Clemens.

The tombstone, made to Sellers' specifications, accompanied him on his riverboat travels for a number of years before his death. It is claimed that once a map of the Mississippi River was carved on the base of the tombstone; if so, age has obliterated it.

Mausoleum Row

Imposing mausoleums were a fashionable status symbol in this period of elaborate mourning customs. Bellefontaine Cemetery abounds with them. And most of them are very impressive. A number are complete with mosaics and/or stained glass windows, handsome iron work, superb stone carvings. A few are even furnished with oriental rugs, carved wood benches, silver urns and the like.

Mausoleum of George Warren Brown (1853-1921) founder of the Brown Shoe Company. The George Warren Brown School of Social Science at Washington University was named in his honor. Inscription above door: "God Hath Given us Eternal Life."

The Lemp Mausoleum is the cemetery's largest as well as one of its most stately mausoleums.

The Lemp Brewery, source of the family fortune, and the city's oldest brewery as well at one time its biggest, is no longer in existence. For the Lemp family, although wealthy and socially prominent, was beset with tragedies and does not have living descendents.

The Lemp mansion, although palatial for its times, is presently a restaurant. In its basement is a stronghold room said to have held as much as twelve-million dollars in cash on occasion, as Mr. William Lemp, Sr., president of the brewery for many years and the family patriarch, did not trust banks as a safe place for keeping money.

Wainwright Tomb, commissioned in 1893 by Elias Wainwright for his recently deceased young wife, Charlotte. Designed by Louis Sullivan, master architect, the tomb is one of the nation's finest works of its kind.

Note the lace-like stone carvings which decorate the entire edifice. The interior, which never sees the light of day, has a fine mosaic ceiling. It seems a pity for such beauty to be forever hidden away.

In the event of the tomb's destruction by either vandalism, earthquake or other disaster, funds in trust for its repair are held in a downtown bank.

A secret lock is concealed in the bronze doors of the Wainwright tomb.

Gothic-style tomb of Adolphus Busch (1842-1913), and his wife Lily (1845-1928), daughter of Eberhard Anheuser, brewer. Busch, who became his father-in-law's partner, developed the Anheuser-Busch Brewery into the world's largest (and still maintained as such by his descendents).

Motto over Busch tomb entrance: "Veni, Vidi, Vici" (I came, I saw, I conquered) is a good description of Busch's character.

Close-up of medieval style baptismal font that decorates exterior of Busch tomb.

A flock of wild geese have set up a permanent home on the chapel lake.

Calvary Cemetery

Likewise laid out in a parklike fashion with winding roads and many trees, Calvary Cemetery has a Tuscan bell tower and several beautiful statues by noted sculptors which further enhance the grounds. Its first mausoleum built for general public use (there are now two), in a tranquil lake setting, with a jewel-like chapel, glorious mosaics and stained glass windows with messages of comfort, is one of Saint Louis' loveliest buildings. And, although seldom visited nowadays except in times of bereavement, it stands high on the list of local treasures.

Decorative mausoleum door.

Although no longer used, the Tuscany bell tower adds an extra note of somber dignity to the cemetery grounds.

Entrance to the Pierre Chouteau family plot. The grave of Madame Chouteau (1733-1814), mother of Pierre and Auguste, first white woman to live in Saint Louis (she arrived in the summer of 1764) and known as **La Mere de Saint Louis** *is here.*

During the years that the Louisiana Territory belonged to Spain, the law required that all citizens must be of the Roman Catholic faith. Thus, many graves of the first Saint Louisans, now in Calvary Cemetery, were moved here from old Catholic cemeteries that were abandoned as the growing city required the land.

Sarcophagus of Charles and Victoire Chouteau Gratiot. Mrs. Gratiot (1760-1823) was one of Madame Chouteau's (and Pierre Laclede's) three daughters. Husband Charles (1752-1817), prominent merchant and fur trader, was a powerful influence in persuading the French villagers of Saint Louis to aid the American cause in the Revolutionary War and, later, in reconciling them to their new American citizenship after the 1804 Louisiana Purchase.

Footnote: It is often forgotten that had it not been for the daring capture from the English on July 4, 1778, of Fort Kaskaskia, and the small towns of Kaskaskia and Cahokia by a rugged band of soldiers led by George Rogers Clark, the boundary between the United States and Canada in this part of North America would probably be the Mississippi River. The help of American-sympathizing Saint Louisans was of inestimable help in the lasting success of this venture, an enormously important episode of the American Revolution.

Tomb of Thomas and Anne Mullanphy Biddle (see page 80).
Designed by George I. Barnett and modeled (except for cross on pediment) after the ancient Temple of the Winds, it was the first tomb of its kind in Saint Louis. Originally on the grounds of the orphanage at Tenth and Biddle Streets founded by Mrs. Biddle, the structure was moved here in 1881.

Preskevia, Queen of the Gypsies, whose funeral in 1923 attracted hordes of her subjects from all over the country.

Kate Chopin, now regarded as one of the outstanding women authors of her time, is a heroine of present-day feminists who resurrected her writings, most of which had been long out of print. However, Mrs. Chopin's free-spirited women characters made her own life extremely difficult. She was ostracized by former friends; denied membership in the Wednesday Club, a local leading women's cultural club; and publicly condemned across the land by both religious and public leaders upon the publication of her novel **The Awakening** *(1899), the story of a woman's love and physical desires outside of her marriage.*

General William Tecumseh Sherman (1820-1891) is considered one of the two best generals to serve in the Union Army. The other, also claimed by Saint Louis, is, of course, Ulysses S. Grant. The two men and their families were close friends.

Sherman is best remembered in U.S. history for his destructive march through Georgia severing the supply lines of the Confederate Armies, which helped bring about the end of the war; his eloquent statement, "War is hell!"; and his forceful refusal to be considered as the 1884 Republican presidential candidate, "If nominated, I will not accept, if elected, I will not serve."

In civilian life before the war, he was president of the local Lucas Horse Car Line. After the war he was given an expensive house on Garrison Street near Franklin Avenue (then a stylish neighborhood) by grateful citizens. The house was razed in the 1960's.

He and his family eventually left Saint Louis for greater opportunities in the East but he was brought back here for burial. His funeral is said to have been the largest ever held in Saint Louis.

The subject of one of the most famous and far-reaching cases in U.S. Jurisprudence, Dred Scott was born a slave in Virginia, brought to Saint Louis by his owners and then taken by them to free territory. When he was brought back to Saint Louis, still a slave, Abolitionists—testing the Missouri Compromise—sued, claiming that Scott's long-time residence in free territory made him a free man.

The case dragged on for ten years and was finally lost in the U.S. Supreme Court. That decision helped to trigger the Civil War. The Fourteenth Amendment of the U.S. Constitution, on which so much twentieth-century social legislation has been based, would probably not have been written so as to confer U.S. citizenship on all persons born in the United States had it not been for this case.

THOMAS A. DOOLEY III, M.D.
JAN. 17, 1927 - JAN. 18, 1961
FOUNDER OF MEDICO

LEGION OF MERIT U.S.A. 1955
OFFICER DE L'ORDER NATIONAL DE VIET NAM 1955
OFFICER OF THE ROYAL ORDER OF THE MILLION ELEPHANTS
AND THE WHITE PARASOL 1959
GRAND OFFICER OF THE ROYAL ORDER OF THE MILLION
ELEPHANTS AND THE WHITE PARASOL 1961
CRISS AWARD 1959
CHRISTOPHER AWARD 1956
CHRISTOPHER AWARD 1961
SPECIAL CONGRESSIONAL MEDAL

AWARDED POSTHUMOUSLY 1962

"THE WOODS ARE LOVELY, DARK AND DEEP,
BUT I HAVE PROMISES TO KEEP,
AND MILES TO GO BEFORE I SLEEP."
ROBERT FROST

Venerated by many for his humanitarian work among the poor and dispossessed in Laos, Vietnam, Cambodia and Malaysia, Dr. Thomas A. Dooley III (1927-1961) received many national and international honors, including (posthumously) the Congressional Medal of Honor, this country's highest award.

He was a founder of Medico (Medical International Cooperation Organization) which, through Dooley's efforts, trained enough medics and nurses to staff seventeen clinics in ten different undeveloped or war-torn countries. (Medico was later absorbed by Care.)

The Robert Frost poem on his tombstone was Dooley's favorite and one he always quoted at the conclusion of his frequent fund-raising lectures.

Dooley's gravesite is still frequently visited by admirers from around the world.

The need and desire to pay tribute to the dead is as old as the human race. Ancient burials offer to archeologists the best and most informative records of the quality and achievements of these previous civilizations. But at the present time, with the changing fashions, no longer are there such grandiose memorials as were customary in the Victorian and Edwardian eras. It will be noted that almost all of the examples used to illustrate this section of *Saint Louis Treasures* are from earlier periods. Present customs call for relatively simple individual tombstones or family plot markers for even the most prominent and wealthy.

Religious Art Treasures

Stone carving of Saint Luke
Christ Church Cathedral Altar Screen
Artist: Harry Helms.
(Christ Church Parish, established 1819,
was the first Protestant Episcopal
parish in the territory from the
Mississippi River to the Pacific Ocean.)

One of mankind's deepest and most compelling instincts has always been the channelling of his finest artistic talents into the creating of objects of veneration and building fitting houses of worship to honor his diety—or dieties.

Saint Louis is no exception. Gloriously beautiful churches, synagogues, temples, all filled with religious objects of inspirational beauty, spiritual import, and often of considerable historic interest too, are to be found throughout the entire area.

Flemish polychrome Madonna and Child
Late thirteenth century
Saint Louis Priory Church.

Seat of altar chair, one of four, expressing various aspects of Judaism.
Temple Emmanuel.
Seat covering is a depiction in needlework art of symbols signifying important Jewish rituals:
Upper left, the shofar; lower left, kiddish cup; center, Ark of the Covenant; lower right, Torah scroll.
The Hand of God (top), the birds and fish, are details copied from the mosaics of the fourth century C.E. (Common Era) Beth Alpha Synagogue excavated in Israel in the 1950's.

Chalice
Trinity Lutheran Church
1805 South Eighth Street.

Jeweled chalice brought to Saint Louis in 1839 by a group of Lutherans from Saxony, Germany, who came here seeking religious freedom. This group became the nucleus of the Missouri Lutheran Synod, one of the largest Lutheran bodies in the world.

The oral tradition concerning this chalice is that it was given to the group by a member of one of the ruling families of Germany in lieu of his coming. An heirloom of the donor, it had been a part of his family's treasures since being brought from Spain several generations earlier.

Painting of part of the Saxon group arriving on the Saint Louis levee February 19, 1839. In the background is the Selma, one of the four steamboats that brought them from New Orleans after their long, hazardous ocean journey to the U.S. in sailing ships.
Artist: G. H. Hilmer
Location: Concordia Seminary Museum.

145

Solid silver monstrance used by Father Marquette
Saint Stanislaus Museum.
In 1673 Marquette and Louis Joliet, the first white men to explore
the Mississippi River, established the existence of a waterway
between the Saint Lawrence River and the Gulf of Mexico.

    Marquette makes no mention of what was to become Saint
Louis, then just wilderness, but his diary notes the Piasa bird
painted on the cliffs near what is now Alton, Illinois, thirty-miles
north of Saint Louis.

    Inasmuch as throughout its entire colonial period, Spanish law required that all citizens of the Louisiana Territory be Roman Catholic, it is axiomatic that the early history of Saint Louis is closely tied to that of the Roman Catholic Church.

First Church Bell in Saint Louis
Old Cathedral Museum.
Formally baptized on December 24, 1774, the bell was named in honor of the popular Spanish governor of Upper Louisiana, Don Pedro Piernas, and his wife, Felicite.

    The bell rang out the angelus thrice daily; summoned the villagers to all important events; tolled out deaths and weddings.

Shrine of Old Saint Ferdinand
Florissant.
Oldest Catholic church building still standing between the Mississippi River and the Rocky Mountains. The present structure was built in 1821 to replace the 1789 log church. The steeple was added in the 1870's.

    Hub of the village for many years, Saint Ferdinand's Church also served as the focal point of the Indian missionary movement of the nineteenth century. Father DeSmet, the most famous of all the missionaries, was ordained here in 1827 and called it home.

    In the early 1960's when no longer a functioning parish church, it was saved from demolition and restored by The Friends of Old Saint Ferdinand's, a non-sectarian group. The building now plays an active role in the City of Florissant's successful efforts to maintain its historic past.

Rock Hill Presbyterian Church, one of the area's oldest churches still functioning in its original edifice, was built by slaves in 1845 on land that was a gift to the newly formed congregation by John and James Marshall. The Marshall brothers, who migrated here from Maryland in the 1820's, once owned almost all of what is now Webster Groves north of Lockwood Avenue.

The popular and influential Reverend Artemus Bullard was on hand for the church's dedication in August, 1845. Mindful of his uncomfortable ride out from the city, he suggested the name "Rock Hill" for the new church—which became the name of the entire community as well as that of most of the Old Military Road which connects Jefferson Barracks to Manchester Road.

Although Spanish law prohibited any but Catholics from settling in Upper Louisiana, by the 1790's, the Spanish governors, wishing to attract the hard-working American pioneers of Protestant stock, made them generous land grants, concessions on their meeting houses and overlooked their ministers' visits, until the latter, were safely back in Illinois territory.

But not until 1817 was the first Protestant church formally organized in Saint Louis. Then there was a spate of them. Presbyterian, Baptist, Methodist, Episcopalian. All by 1820. The first black congregation (Baptist) was formed in 1822; the first Jewish congregation in 1836.

John Clark Tombstone, Coldwater Cemetery.
The first Protestant minister in Upper Louisiana, Clark would slip stealthily into the territory after dark and return to Illinois by dawn, in order to prevent being arrested by Spanish authorities.

Hungry for Protestant sermons, his little congregations would quietly come to an agreed-upon meeting place and spend the night listening to Clark's exhortations.

Early nineteenth-century needlepoint tapestry (circa 1820's) of Leonardo da Vinci's "The Last Supper"
First Presbyterian Church
Artist: Sarah Hempstead Beebe, one of the seven founders of the First Presbyterian Church in 1817.
The work was returned to the church through the oddest of coincidences by a California descendent who was unaware of the part his ancestress played in the establishment of the First Presbyterian Church of Saint Louis.

Fabergé Easter Egg created for the Czar of Russia. Executed by Feodor Ruecket, chief enameller in the Fabergé Establishment.
Kluender Collection Concordia Seminary Library.

The Reverend Paul and Lydia Kluender Collection of Russian Religious Art had its origin at the time that he served as pastor in a Chicago church in whose congregation were a number of White Russian émigrés. In payment for his services to them, he would often be given their religious art objects. The Kluenders continued to enlarge their collection over the years.

The collection is composed of a number of Russian Easter eggs, many of them Fabergé creations; ikons, some dating back to the thirteenth century; ancient paintings and other miscellaneous (often highly unusual) art objects. In the 1960's the Kluenders gave the entire collection to the Concordia Lutheran Seminary with the stipulation that some of the collection always be on view.

Interior of a triptych, another Fabergé Easter Egg. The figure in the center is the Triumphant Christ; on left, is Mary, Mother of Jesus; on the right, the Angel Gabriel.
Kluender Collection Concordia Seminary Library.

The Ascension
Oak Grove Mausoleum.

Tiffany stained glass window from the former Church of the Ascension (Episcopal) which stood at Cates and Goodfellow Avenues. Although a number of local city churches have very fine Tiffany windows that were also executed at the time that Louis Tiffany's genius was at its peak, this is the largest. It was saved from destruction by the Stanza brothers of Oak Grove Cemetery when the church was torn down (Tiffany windows were out of fashion at the time and the expense of moving the window and recreating it in a proper setting did not seem worthwhile to any others). Depicting the ascension of Jesus in a cloud of glory as some of his awe-struck followers look on, the window now ennobles their mausoleum. As it faces south, visitors should seek to see the window on the afternoon of a sunny day when its beauty is dazzling.

Sanctuary, whose baldachino is said to be surpassed in magnificence only by that of Saint Peter's in Rome.

Cathedral of Saint Louis, King of France

Architects: Barnett, Hayes and Barnett   Mosaics: Ravenna Company.

Inspired by the Hagia Sophia built in 532 A.D. in Istanbul (then Constantinople) by Emperor Justinian, the Cathedral of Saint Louis, King of France, is acknowledged world-wide as one of the great churches of Christendom. Its interior, as an expression of Byzantine architecture, is without parallel in the Western Hemisphere.

Begun in 1907, dedicated in 1914, work on the cathedral has been continuous ever since. Not until 1985 were the mosaics, one of its chief glories, finished. And, as in medieval times, working on the mosaics has been the life-work of some artisans.

Hidden in a dark corridor by All Souls' Chapel is this mosaic head of Jesus as a young man, inspired by ancient pictures of him when he was usually shown clean-shaven. After about 600 A.D., Jesus was almost always portrayed with a beard.

Louis IX's mother, Blanche of Castile, granddaughter of Henry II of England and Eleanor of Aquitaine, was his chief advisor until her death in 1252. (And also probably one of the world's most difficult mothers-in-law.)

Mosaics in the narthex depicting scenes from the life of Louis IX (Saint Louis), King of France. (1226-1270 A.D.).

Head of Saint Jerome, one of four mosaic portraits of the founders of the Western Christian Church, on altar beneath the baldachino.

Louis IX is considered the ideal medieval Christian monarch. Pious, concerned about his people's welfare and a good administrator, he was the leader of the Seventh Crusade (1248-54) and undertook the Eighth Crusade (1270) which was cut short by his death. To be a leader of a crusade was the highest honor of his time.

151

Mosaics illustrating a portion of the beatitudes. The others face these on the opposite side of the cathedral. In the right background is All Souls' Chapel.

Bronze, bejeweled cross over main exit door of sanctuary. Dating back to the second century A.D., it is one of the oldest Christian relics in the U.S.

During the period that Emperor Justinian was building the Hagia Sophia, it was the custom to use building materials from outlawed pagan temples in the construction of the many new Christian churches being built throughout the Roman Empire.

Thus, Justinian made use of pillars from a variety of sources, all of different kinds and colors of marble with dissimilar carved capitals taken from destroyed pagan houses of worship. This plan was followed in the St. Louis Cathedral; hence the pillars are made of varied marble and unalike capitals.

The art of the Western World during the Medieval Ages and the Renaissance when the power of the Christian Church was at its zenith, was primarily a form of sacred writing. And like all written languages, it had to be learned in order to be understood. The spiritual messages to be conveyed were in the stained glass windows, the paintings, the statues, carved into the pews and roof beams, and the stone exteriors of the churches. Almost everything that could be called art in any form carried some kind of a religious message—all of which had meaning for the general populace. Today, because this symbolic language is no longer taught, almost all of these messages have been forgotten by the great majority—even devout church-goers.

The flaming north red rose window of the cathedral is a case in point. Unfortunately, the window itself is obscured by the baldachino and can only be seen from two vantage points in the church. But the spiritual message it carries is an important one to all Christians. The enormous Greek cross surrounded by thorns is symbolic of Jesus' death on the cross; the meandering grapevine is a symbol of the ever-presence of God; the two drinking harts representing the faithful seeking God, is based on Psalm 42: 1, "As a hart panteth after the water brooks so panteth my soul after thee, oh God."

The design of the surrounding wall with its blue background was derived from the world-famous fifth-century mausoleum of the Empress Galla Placidia in Ravenna, Italy, which was then capital of the Western Roman Empire.

To the left is the mosaic dome of the baldachino.

Mosaic: Pontius Pilate and Jesus, King of the Jews
Saint John's Mercy Hospital Chapel
Artist: Robert Harmon.

Eighteenth-century Russian ikon of the Christ Child
Paul and Lydia Kluender Russian Religious Art Collection
Concordia Seminary Library.

Hand-carved statue of Saint Elizabeth of Hungary, a much-loved saint of the Slovak peoples
Saint John Nepomuk Church South Eleventh Street.

It, along with the statues of several other popular Middle European religious personages, was imported from Bohemia in the 1870's to adorn the church. All continue to give Saint John Nepomuk Church a distinctive ethnic character.

"Come Unto Me" Chancel Window (Tiffany)
Second Presbyterian Church Westminster Place.

This is one of a number of the Tiffany windows (along with others by noted artists) that beautify the sanctuary of Second Presbyterian Church.

Like all truly fine stained glass windows, they are a wondrous sight to behold and elicit a fervent hosanna from the spirit. Especially on a bright day with the sunlight streaming through them bringing out their rich, glowing colors.

Sanctuary, Saint Nicholas Greek Orthodox Church.

The Saint Nicholas Greek Orthodox Church, the largest of several Eastern Rite Orthodox churches in Saint Louis (it belongs to the Ecumenical Patriarchate, Istanbul, Turkey) was established in 1917 when there were finally enough Greeks in the locality to support a church. That same year a small building was purchased for their worship purposes. A much larger church edifice was built in 1931 at the present location on Forest Park Boulevard. In 1961, to meet still further growth and expanding needs of the congregation, a new community center was built and the church itself considerably enlarged.

Among local churches, the Saint Nicholas sanctuary is second only to the Saint Louis Cathedral in the golden splendor of its magnificence. One of the imposing chandeliers was the gift of Spyros Skouras, the highly successful movie mogul, once an active member here.

(A long-standing quarrel between the Eastern and Western (Church of Rome) branches of Christianity finally came to a head in 1054 with both church bodies excommunicating the other. A reconciliation of sorts of this nearly a thousand-year old rift is only now being effected in these last decades of the twentieth century.)

To explore historic South Side and North Side churches is to turn the clock back to a time when European nationals were flooding into Saint Louis to seek the many opportunities offered in the United States with its "gold-paved streets," to escape the political and religious oppressions of the Old World, its constant wars and the military service required of all young males.

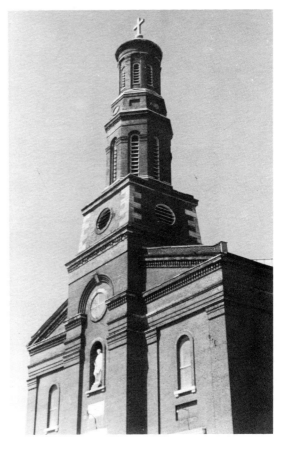

Saint Vincent de Paul Church (1844)
Architect: Meriwether Clark, eldest son of General William Clark
Location: Ninth and Park Streets.
Built on land given to Bishop Rosati of the Saint Louis Roman Catholic Diocese by Madame Julie Soulard, widow of Antoine Soulard, Surveyor-General of Alta Luisiana. This land was part of an enormous land grant given to Soulard by the Spanish governors in lieu of cash for his services.

The land grant was long in litigation as to the family's right of ownership. Not until the mid-1830's when this was finally established by a Supreme Court decision was the Soulard Area opened for settlement. Saint Vincent de Paul Church, the first church of any denomination to be built here, was for the accommodation of the large numbers of newly arrived German Catholics streaming into this part of the city to begin their lives in the New World.

Shrine of Saint Joseph
Eleventh and Biddle Streets.
On land donated by Mrs. Anne Biddle, the first Saint Joseph's Church was built in 1844. Expansive growth of the area made it necessary to enlarge the church in 1866 and again in 1880 (the present church).

Saint Joseph's famed Altar of Answered Prayers, given by grateful parishioners for the cessation of deaths in the devastating 1866 cholera epidemic, is a replica of the Altar of Saint Ignatius in the Jesuit Gesu Church in Rome, except for the substitution of the silver statues of Saint Joseph and the Child Jesus for that of Ignatius.

Faced with demolition in the 1970's, the church was saved by a group of dedicated, non-sectarian laymen. One of the city's most beautiful historic churches, Saint Joseph's is gradually being restored to its former grandeur. Now in the center of a revitalized neighborhood, it is once more flourishing and meeting the spiritual needs of many.

Saint Alphonsus (Rock) Church 1867
1118 North Grand Boulevard.

The twenty large stained glass windows that form most of the north and south walls of the church are of breath-taking beauty. Especially on a sunny day. Because of these windows, installed in the 1890's, the church was one of the German exhibits of the 1904 World's Fair.

Its Mother of Perpetual Help Shrine is venerated by local Catholics and thousands have come here to pray before it. The holy eleventh-century ikon, of which this is an exact copy, is at Saint Alphonsus Church in Rome.

A number of the surviving old churches have glorious stained glass windows, many of which were imported in the late nineteenth century from Germany, Bavaria or Czechoslovakia (this was a high-water mark period for excellence in stained glass in these countries).

It is an impossible task to adequately describe the beauty of these windows — or picture them in black and white. They are truly among the city's greatest treasures.

Nativity Scene, one of a number of equally magnificent windows at Saint John Nepomuk Church, first Czechoslovakian Church in the U.S. (1859) and Mother Church of all other Czech churches in this country. This building dates from the late 1890's.

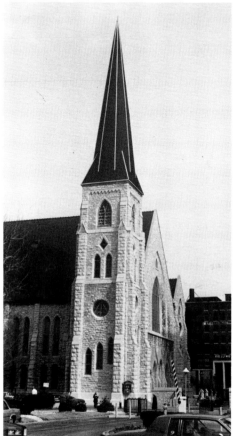

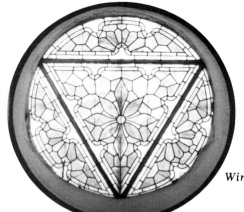

Window, Centenary Methodist Church

Centenary United Methodist Church, Sixteenth and Pine Streets, founded in 1839, was named in honor of the founding of Methodism (1739) by John Wesley at Oxford, England.

The present building, dating from 1869, is one of the city's oldest Protestant congregations still using the same church edifice for worship purposes.

159

Holy Ark, Shaare Zedek Synagogue.
The elaborate silver crown (kesser) atop the Torah scroll on the right signifies that the Torah is king. The two ceremonial objects (rimmonims) that adorn the Torah on the left have little bells that tinkle as the holy scrolls pass amongst the congregation signaling all to stand in their honor.

The breast-plate, symbolic of Aaron's, worn by the high priest of old, is a symbol that the Torah is now the supreme authority in God's relation to man.

Judaism, as do all religions, has a rich symbolic language to express its precepts and beliefs. And, like all symbols, they must be understood in order to have meaning.

The center of every Jewish synagogue or temple is the Ark, representing the Ark of the Covenant in which were kept the tablets of stone on which the Ten Commandments were written. The Ark today in all Jewish Houses of Worship holds the Torah or Holy Word of God. In front of the Ark burns a lamp (the eternal light) to signify the ever-presence of God.

Chapel Window Shaare Zedek Synagogue
Artist: Rodney Winfield.
Three-dimensional window based on symbols relating to the Book of Exodus, a heritage shared by both the Jewish and Christian faiths.
The dominant glowing red figuration symbolizes the burning bush from which God spoke to Moses giving him directions for taking his people out of bondage. The pyramids represent the years of servitude in Egypt; the serpent, the rod that Moses picked up and which then became a serpent; the doorpost, with the Mezzuzah and lamb's blood, protecting the first-born of the Israelites; and the waves, the parting of the Red Sea through which Moses finally led his people to safety from the avenging Pharaoh.

To look at this window and understand its message is a lesson in early monotheism.

Altar
Temple Israel
Artist: Rodney Winfield.
A great deal of the history of the early Israelites is encompassed in this high altar. The large center object symbolizes the "pillar of cloud by day and of fire by night" that lead them safely through the desert to the Promised Land; the Ten Commandments are found in every synagogue but these are turned upside down to signify the first tables of stone which Moses broke in anger when he discovered his people worshipping the golden calf; the Ark of the Covenant, a simple wooden box, denotes their early nomadic habits; the menorah, the seven-branched candlestick, the light of learning. The pulpit on the right side of the altar, represents the wailing wall, all that is left of Solomon's Temple destroyed by the Romans in 70 A.D. The other altar objects have similar symbolic meanings important in Judiasm.

As Judaic religious laws forbid the use of the human form in its art, much of Jewish religious artistry finds expression in rich Torah coverings such as these from Temple Emmanuel.

One of twelve needlepoint pictures, B'Nai Amoona synagogue, which were inspired by the renowned Chagall windows in the Medical Center Synagogue, Hadassah Hebrew University, Jerusalem. Each represents one of the tribes of Judah which were blessed by Jacob.

As in all religious iconography, trees, animals and foliage all have religious significance. The fish in the above symbolizes the Tribe of Zebulon, the child of Leah, "who dwelt in the haven of the sea and was a haven for ships."

The needlepoint pictures were created by women of the B'Nai Amoona Congregation.

Church of the Most Holy Trinity, Fourteenth and Mallinckrodt Streets.
The parish was first established in 1848 to take care of the rapidly growing
Catholic-German population in the section of North Saint Louis known as Baden,
founded by Edward Mallinckrodt, Sr. (of Mallinckrodt Chemical Company).
Present edifice dates from 1885.

For centuries—until the advent of modern architecture after World War II, Christian churches of the Western World usually proclaimed themselves as Houses of God by steeples thrust into the air. Saint Louis has many that are a joy to behold, a delight to the eye.

Trinity Presbyterian Church, University City.

Saint Mark's United Methodist Church, Florissant.

Christ Church Cathedral Belfry
Thirteenth and Locust Streets
Architect: Kevis Tully.
   Gothic-style tower added to the 1859 structure in 1912. Note gargoyles (called fascinators in medieval times) to ward off evil spirits.

Originally the Church of the Messiah (Unitarian) built in 1880. William Greenleaf Eliot, a founder of Washington University and Mary Institute, was also founder of the church (1835) and its pastor for many years. T. S. Eliot, the famous poet, was his grandson and attended this church as a boy.
   Sold by the Unitarians in 1907, the building passed through the hands of several denominations. Now burned and gutted, about all that remains is its splendorous steeple adorning the skyline.
Garrison and Locust Streets.

Saint Peter's Episcopal Church   Ladue
Architect: Guy Study.
Although built since the advent of contemporary architecture, this church is a reversion to colonial church architecture with its steeple being typical of those that dot the skys of New England.

Holy Redeemer Church   Webster Groves
Architect: A. Stauder.
A modern version of the steeple; note the serendipitous bell shadows on the church wall.

163

Saint Mark's Episcopal Church   4717 Clifton Avenue   Architects: Nagel and Dunn.

In retrospect, one of Saint Louis' most historic churches is Saint Mark's Episcopal Church for it was a national forerunner of the functionally designed religious edifice. Built in 1939, it was the second church in all of the Americas to be built in a utilitarian type of architecture and to break away from the traditional Gothic, white-steepled Colonial - or even occasional Greek Revival - styles. These were all considered eminently appropriate for houses of worship of every faith.

Although economy (and the bishop's order) dedicated its form rather than the desire of Saint Mark's congregation to be in the vanguard of modern architecture (they hated it), the nation-wide publicity that the church engendered for its stark simplicity brought it to the attention of thousands across the United States, and it is now considered an important style-setter for contemporary church architecture.

Ethical Society of St. Louis' Meeting Hall
Architect: Harris Armstrong.
The Ethical Society has always been of great influence in the cultural life of the community. Roger Baldwin, founder of the American Civil Liberties Union, was once a member of this congregation.

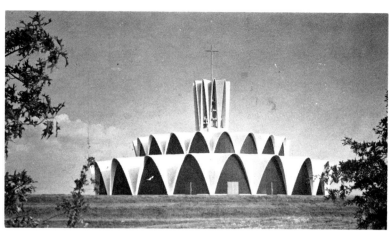

Church of the Saint Louis Priory
Architect: Gyo Obato.
The Priory is a community of English Benedictine monks invited to Saint Louis by a local Catholic group to start a new boys' preparatory school.
    The architectural design of their church has won numerous awards and is one of the most photographed churches in America.

During the 1950's, '60's and '70's a tremendous number of new houses of worship of modern architectural designs were constructed across the land. This was the result of the prosperity of the period coinciding with a need for new religious expressions, as many of the older churches and synagogues seemed hopelessly out of date in this wave of contemporary architecture. And, perhaps most important of all, the shifting of large numbers of the population to recently developed areas which then required new buildings for religious purposes. Most of these were designed in the new popular modern styles.

Because of Saint Mark's Episcopal Church, Saint Louis was a part of this movement from its onset. And the result is a rather large number of religious edifices of contemporary architecture. Some, strikingly handsome, add considerable luster to local architectural stock.

Former B'Nai Amoona Synagogue   University City
Architect: Eric Mendelsohn.
Mendelsohn, a famous German-Jewish expressionist architect fled Nazi Germany to escape persecution. His first commission in the United States was the B'Nai Amoona Synagogue (built 1949).
    In recent years, B'Nai Amoona Synagogue, following most of its congregation's moving to suburbs further west, has built a new synagogue and sold this distinguished building which is now to be used for secular purposes.

Memorial Chapel, Jefferson Barracks National Cemetery, is the only chapel in any of the 109 National Cemeteries. Here it serves a very real need for funeral services in an enclosed harmonious building for members of the armed forces.

Non-sectarian and initiated by the Gold Star wives and mothers of Saint Louis, the chapel was built in 1977 by congressional appropriation. However, all projects to further enhance the chapel—stained glass windows with symbols of every faith, sculpture, organ, etc., have been paid for by private resources.

Kirkwood Methodist Church
Architect: Leslie Black.
Although a long-time church congregation in Kirkwood (founded 1867), this building was constructed in 1964 to meet present-day needs.

The church was built to resemble an upturned ship, an ancient symbol for safety and security. Nave, the word for a church sanctuary, comes from the Latin word navis, meaning ship.

Temple Emmanuel
Architect: William Bernoudy, trained by Frank Lloyd Wright.
Exterior is designed in the form of the Star of David. The sanctuary, inspired by Wright's famous Unity Temple, has a high degree of warmth and intimacy, qualities not too often found in religious edifices.

Artist: Robert Harmon
Executed by the Emil Frei Company
Location: Faith Salem United Church of Christ.
Salem Church, founded in 1877, merged with Faith Church in 1948. Present building erected 1954.

    Entire north wall of church is one large window divided into panels, each with a Christian message.

    Illustrated: Isaiah's prophecy of the coming Messiah: "Unto us a child is born, unto us a son is given; and the government shall be upon his shoulder; and his name shall be called Wonderful, Counseller, The Mighty God, The Everlasting Father, The Prince of Peace." (Is. 9:6)

    Hand represents the hand of God "the giver of every good gift and every perfect gift." (Jas. 1:17)

Artist: Siegfried Reinhardt
Executed by the Emil Frei Company
Location: Second Baptist Church, founded 1832, present building 1957.
Inscription: "Seek ye first the kingdom of God and His righteousness and all these things shall be added unto you." (Matt. 7:33)

A substantially large number of the windows that beautify churches and synagogues in this section of the United States have been made by the century-old Emil Frei Company of Saint Louis, whose fame for the excellence of its stained glass artistry is international.

Like a great deal of religious art—both ancient and modern—these windows need explaining in order for their message to be fully understood.

Artist: Robert Harmon
Executed by the Emil Frei Company
Location: Kirkwood United Methodist Church.
One of the six windows depicting the story of creation as related in the first chapter of Genesis. "In the beginning God created the heaven and the earth. And the earth was without form and void; and darkness was upon the face of the deep. And the Spirit of God moved upon the face of the waters." (Gen 1:1-3)

Stone carving of the lamb carrying the cross, an oft-used Christian symbol of Jesus triumphant, on an exterior wall of Grace Methodist Church, Skinker Boulevard and Waterman Avenue.

The church, built in 1892, formerly stood at Lindell Boulevard and Newstead Avenue, an area then called Piety Row because of the many churches there. To follow its congregation westward, the building was torn down in 1913 and moved—stone by stone—to its present location.

Pictured on this and the following two pages is only a paltry smattering of the many religious art objects of historical interest, exquisite workmanship and spiritual beauty to be found in various Saint Louis houses of worship. The total numbers are staggering and well-worthy of an entire book being devoted to them.

Celtic Cross
Trinity Presbyterian Church, University City.
Its beauty in its simplicity, this large, high-lighted cross dominates the altar of Trinity Presbyterian Church and is the focal point of the sanctuary.

The Celtic Cross is the style of cross most often used by Presbyterian churches across the world. It was in common usage in the British Isles prior to the coming of Augustine in 597 A.D. who imposed Roman Catholic rule upon the islands.

After the Reformation, it was re-adopted by Presbyterian groups to signify that their early Christian heritage had roots of its own that had no connection with the Church of Rome.

Christus Rex Crucifix (Jesus triumphant over death)
Artist: Victor Berlandis
Location: Holy Trinity Episcopal Church.
Jesus' message of eternal life was a prime factor in the rapid growth of Christianity throughout the Western World in the early centuries after his death. This style of crucifix is now often used in Episcopal churches to proclaim this great promise.

Mosaic altar with Saint Raymond, patron saint of church, as the central figure
Saint Raymond's Marionite Church
931 Lebanon Drive.
Church founded in the early twentieth century by Lebanese immigrants who settled in this area. As the years passed and this section of the city deteriorated, almost all of the congregation moved away but continued to support their church. In 1975 a new church was built as part of the Lasalle-Park Restoration.

German baroque, hand-carved wooden pulpit
Trinity Lutheran Church — South Eighth Street.
The church built on this site in 1869 was completely demolished in the 1896 tornado. All that survived the destruction was the pulpit and baptismal font.

   The congregation took this as a sign from on high that all that really mattered was the Word and the Sacraments and immediately set about rebuilding the church with the pulpit and the font having special places of honor.

   A statue of an apostle, damaged beyond repair, was replaced with one of Martin Luther, the gift of a congregation in Germany.

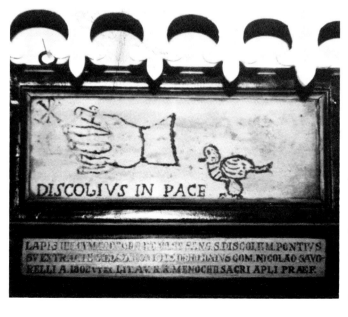

Second-century tombstone taken from the Roman catacombs in 1806 on the mandate of Pope Pius VII is one of the several relics of early martyred Christians given the Mother General of the Sisters of Saint Joseph, Carondelet, on an 1861 visit to Rome. She was able to obtain these for the new Mother House Chapel in Carondelet through a close friendship with the sister of Monsignor Joseph Ferrari, then Treasurer of the Papal States. The authenticity of the relics is verified in an 1807 document executed by Cardinal Somoglia of the Vatican.

Crucifix
Artist: John Angel
Firmin Desloge Hospital Chapel.
Of Gothic revival architecture and inspired by the Sainte-Chapelle made for Louis IX, the chapel was designed by Ralph Adam Cram, the best-known and most impassioned medievalist architect of his time (1930's).

Recently further embellished by vivid stained glass windows, the visitor to the chapel now has the distinct impression of being within a jewel case aglow with precious stones.
Restoration architect: Verner Burks.

Statue of the Archangel Michael combatting Satan
Sculptor: Ernst Grosemann
Entrance to Concordia Seminary Library.
Stored for safekeeping in the salt-mines near Salzburg during World War II, it was brought to this country after the war.

Needlepoint panel picturing events in life of Saint Francis of Assisi
Artists: Gwendolyn Hudson, Lee Herpolschemier
Holy Communion Episcopal Church.

Yad, several centuries old, was given to Shaare Zedek Synagogue by the sole survivor of a German Jewish congregation annihilated in the holocaust.

Going back to his village after the war, he recovered the yad from its hiding place and brought it with him to America.

(A yad is used by the rabbi of every Jewish congregation to follow the words of the Torah as he reads so that his hand does not touch the sacred pages.)

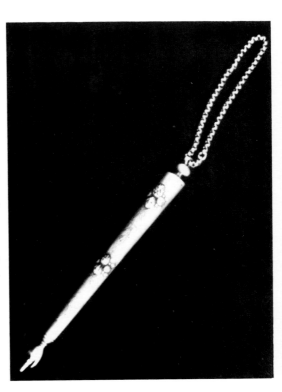

New Treasures
from
Old Treasures

High on a bluff overlooking the Missouri River is graceful Thornhill built by Frederick Bates, Missouri's second governor. Bates, who came to Missouri in 1807 to serve as Secretary of the Louisiana Territory, Recorder of Land Titles, and a member of the Board of Land Commissioners to settle Spanish Land Grant claims, modeled Thornhill after the plantation houses of his home state of Virginia.

In 1824 Bates succeeded Alexander McNair as governor. And although he only served a year before his unexpected death, during this period he wrote many of the first land laws of the state which were eventually to influence the entire settlement of the West.

The house, nine outbuildings and ninety-eight acres of Bates' original estate of nearly a thousand acres, were donated to Saint Louis County in 1968. Several years of historical, archeological and architectural research followed. Restored now to a pristine 1825 condition, this lovely old house and some of the outbuildings are open to the public.

Patterned after the stagecoaches in use at the time, this 1833 Boston and Providence Railroad passenger coach is one of the oldest in existence in the U.S. On display at the National Museum of Transport, Baxter Road, whose collection of transportation vehicles is unmatched anywhere.

First founded in 1944 by Dr. John P. Roberts, a local physician, and privately funded for many years, the museum was taken over by Saint Louis County in 1984. This was with the jubilant consent of all involved because of the additions, improvements and better maintenance of present exhibits that would be possible by its being a part of the county park system.

Powell Hall Foyer
The former Saint Louis Theatre, once a glittering movie and vaudeville house, stood vacant for a number of years. The crowds who formerly attended were long gone and the building was in a wretched condition. In 1968 when the property went up for sale, the Saint Louis Symphony Society realized that, renovated, it would be a splendid showcase for the orchestra.

As the result of a successful fund drive and the generous gift of a million dollars from Mrs. Walter Powell, the dream became a reality. Powell Hall, named in honor of Mrs. Powell's deceased husband, now ranks high on the list of the world's most elegantly beautiful orchestra halls.

Fox Theatre Lobby
The Fox Theatre, built in 1929 to be the crown jewel of William Fox's movie empire, and second in size only to New York's Roxy Theatre, was an exotic stunner. Siamese-Byzantine architecture was the word coined to describe it. But in the course of time it fell on evil days; was closed for lack of attendance and allowed to slump into a deplorable state of disrepair. Until 1980. In that year the theatre was purchased by Mary and Leon Strauss who, with their associates, restored the Fabulous Fox to a lavish grandeur. And here is now being offered some of the best entertainment in the U.S.

173

Brand New Treasures

An entrance to the Saint Louis Centre, the three-story, three-blocks-long shopping mall connecting Saint Louis' two largest department stores.

All of glass and steel supports, bright, airy and cheerful, its design patterned after the famed Crystal Palace of London's Great 1851 Exposition, the mall is playing a vital role in city's rejuvenation plans of bringing crowds back to the downtown areas.

Flanked by houses of traditional styles, the design of this new addition to the row of stately mansions on Lindell Boulevard is heavily influenced by the Bauhaus School of Architecture and Architect Le Corbousier. Needless to say, the daring simplicity of its stark whiteness has made the house the subject of considerable controversy among Saint Louisans. The viewer either admires it wholeheartedly — or the reverse.

Built for Herbert and Marcia Smith, Mrs. Smith is a designer of contemporary interiors.
Architect: Gary Glenn.

Treasure: WEALTH OR RICHES STORED OR ACCUMULATED; WEALTH, RICH MATERIALS OR VALUABLE THINGS; ANYTHING GREATLY VALUED OR HIGHLY PRIZED; TO REGARD OR TREAT AS PRECIOUS, PRIZED, CHERISHED.

*. . . Random House Dictionary of the
English Language.*

Elinor Martineau Coyle   Tower Grove Park Ruins

About The Author

Elinor Martineau Coyle's love affair with Saint Louis began when she came here as a bride. This was at the time when disparaging Saint Louis was almost a civic virtue. So, except for a relatively few other kindred and optimistic souls, it was lonesome going at first.

She says, "I am so grateful for my niche in time for this has given me the rare good fortune of being in on the renaissance of Saint Louis from its earliest days in the late 1950's.

"Now look at what has happened! Everywhere there are new wonders for the city. No longer are its charms hidden away to be discovered only by the earnest seeker. They are there for all to see, to enjoy, to appreciate. This is an exciting and exhilarating period in Saint Louis' history. And a wonderful time for all Saint Louisans with an opportunity to play a part in the rebirth of this great city."

About this book, she continues, "I know I have left out the favorite treasures of many. I even had to omit some of my own for the decisions of what to use—and what not to use—were difficult. And, obviously, there was neither time nor space to recount them all. Especially nowadays when new ones are being created at such a rapid rate. But I do hope that the representative sampling of Saint Louis treasures in this book will be enjoyed by its readers and encourage them to seek out their own for additional pleasures."

Born and reared in Wisconsin, Mrs. Coyle is a descendent of early Wisconsin settlers; her interest in regional history stems from the tales passed down in her family of pioneer days. She is a graduate of the University of Wisconsin; her husband is Charles S. Coyle, a native Saint Louisan.